D1798913

GIDEON:
Releasing The Potentials Within You

Sammy O. Joseph

PPH
Pulse Publishing House

© 2011 Sammy O. Joseph

First published 2001
Revised edition published 2011

Published in the United Kingdom by
Pulse Publishing House
Box 15129
Birmingham
England B45 5DJ

pulsepublishinghouse@harvestways.org

All rights reserved. No part of this publication may be reproduced, stored in a retrieval system, or be transmitted, in any form, or by any means, mechanical, electronic, photocopying or otherwise without prior written consent of the publisher.

Bible quotes are from the King James Version of the Bible unless otherwise stated.

Amplified quotes are from the Amplified Bible, © copyright 1995 by The Zondervan Corporation and The Lockman Foundation.

Cover design by Pulse Publishing House, England.
Typesetting by Wordzworth Limited, London.
Printed in England by Lightning Source UK Ltd.

ISBN 978-0-9567298-2-8

Contents

Acknowledgements

To the young men and women of God called into ministry with me in England, South Africa and Nigeria; *The Harvestways Int'l Church* members, ministry friends and partners; my sons and daughters in the faith who have encouraged, supported and interceded for me in various ways, may Heaven immensely reward you. Without you, I could not have gotten this far.

Together, we will take our rightful places in destiny. I pray for you God's richest blessings this day and always.

SAMMY JOSEPH

Birmingham, England.

Dedication

This book is dedicated to these servants of God for the indelible impact their ministries have had on my formative and preparative ministry years:

Dr. Billy Graham *the foremost American Evangelist in the last century, who gave me the glimpses of what it means to be an Evangelist and a voice of God to the Nations.*

Dr. Chuck Swindoll *whose 'Insight for Living' was a ready companion and reference tool in those years of ministry preparation.*

Prof. A. Imevbore *who discovered me for ministry at a youthful age.*

Bishop (Dr.) Francis Oke *who commissioned The Harvestways International Church.*

To my five best friends and gifts from God: Gabriella, David, Daniel, Priscilla and Paul; thank you for so being patient and understanding when I was busy spending many hours either at study or prayer, on the phone praying with or counseling someone; working on this project — or indeed, consulting with our pastors, giving them directives.

You're indeed, God's amazing, wonderful and finest gifts!

I love you!

Daddy.

Introduction

This package in your hands draws analogies from the life of Gideon (one of Israel's Judges) and applies them to how you can effectively release the hidden potentials within you. Not only this, it combines true life stories, life transforming testimonies and sound words of counsel that will serve as a manual for the growing Christian worker – or indeed a missionary in a faraway land, away from the influence of families and friends.

For you encountering just the pressures of daily routines, I have written expressly, bearing in mind the lessons the Lord had taught me on how you will win over your commonest varied challenges!

It is my essential prayer that you will become all that God created you to be.

Chapter 1

Correct Your Defective Background

"And your ancient ruins shall be rebuilt; you shall raise up the foundations of [buildings that have laid waste for] many generations ..."

- PROPHET ISAIAH

Your background is your root. No matter how evasive you may try to be about it, you will be traced to it, someday.

Any man's background always bears a direct impact upon their destiny depending upon whether that background was *effective* or *defective*. If yours was an effective background, bless the Lord; bless your parents. You must however not rest on the oars of that heritage. You must enhance that positive legacy thereby making it more glorious, that you may bequeath a more beneficial endowment to your posterity.

1

Some others, however, have inherited a legacy not so fortunate. You don't need to either despair or blame anyone. It is such inheritors of lesser-than-effective legacies I hope to address in this entire book.

Notice though, great minds have always been traced *not* to have emerged from the best of backgrounds. Most of them actually have sprouted from more negative roots than otherwise conceived. They, like you and I, were born with potentials buried within their very fabrics. In due time – and with good conscious efforts aimed at nurturing and developing those potentials – the maturity of these inherent giftings should begin to yield huge dividends!

Great people like the scientist Albert Einstein, the English preacher Smith Wigglesworth and the former American President Abraham Lincoln had their dates with destiny because they chose to rise above their limitations. Even some of today's modern 'stars' *did* have *something* said against them, sometime. Few worthy names as Walt Disney of Disneyland, Mike 'Air' Jordan formerly of *Chicago Bulls* and Dr. Ben Carson, the neurosurgeon didn't just hit prominence, except there was a due cause!

'Due Causes' that Result into Prominence

Consider these due causes that helped birth the spurt of accelerated growth in these lives:

Albert Einstein's emotional dysfunction. Albert's youthful teacher said he was emotionally damaged and did not appear to have much intellect. Many years later, Einstein proved his teacher's self-fulfilling prophecy wrong! He emerged the most brilliant mind ever known.

Smith Wigglesworth's disadvantaged background. Smith Wigglesworth was a wrecked illiterate drunk - and yet when the hands of his Creator got hold of him, it became Smith's lifelong calling and assignment to tell of his supernatural encounter and the 'new creation' created out of the ashes of his past. Considered to be unschooled, Wigglesworth re-educated those considered to be the scholars of his time. He crossed the oceans many times, brandishing *his* calling; sharing the simple Gospel of Jesus Christ!

'What cannot the Creator God do with you if you would awaken your sleeping giant, roll up your sleeves – and invest your time and efforts at discovering and polishing your hidden potentials?'

Abraham Lincoln's repeated attempts at the Presidency. History records how Abraham Lincoln failed repeatedly before clinching his dream and becoming the 16th American President. That feat took him a total of almost three decades.

Walt Disney's lack of 'creativity'. This should jolt you; it did me when I first learned of it: Walt Disney was *"fired"* by his *Mickey Mouse* employers because they said he was *not* creative enough!

Are you still listening to the 'nay-sayers'?

3

And do you know that Mike Jordan was turned down in High School by the Basketball Team because the coach said his skills weren't sharp enough?

Do you know that Ben Carson was referred to as the "class dummy" in his class? Raised in impoverishment by a single mom with poor grades, a tempestuous rage and low self esteem, despite these defective circumstances, Ben obtained great success; he became the best, in his field of endeavor!

The secret of his success laid in a godly, praying and hard-working mom, Sonya – who though herself was limited to just the third grade education inculcated in young Ben and his brother Curtis, the love of learning. Sonya cut down the hours the boys spent behind the TV for the local library – where they were mandated to write weekly book reports. Though she couldn't read them; she pretended to absorb her boys' budding, developing inner giftings. The whole world knows today, Sonya Carson was correct!

Walt Disney, Mike Jordan, Dr. Ben Carson – and the like *did* prove their critics wrong.

Isn't it your turn to overrule the predictions of the 'naysayers' in your life?

Dig in Deep; Don't quit. Work at your Potential

People who had come to fully release their potentials *had not* quitted when the going got tough. Rather, one quality had they in common: perseverance!

For them, caving in, giving up and quitting are not viable options to choose from.

Like in aerobic exercises, physical muscles – much like character – are best formed under the application of great pressure.

When the pressures of life deluge you like a broken dam, you too must learn to dig in deep, maintain focus – and not quit! Aiming a title-winning shot must be your goal. Be positive. Apostle Paul says: *"I can do all things through Christ which strengtheneth me."* [1]

If you missed the mark, don't complain. Quit playing the *blame game*. Prepare. Aim again – and shoot! You surely will hit your target. You will succeed.

You may be saying: *'Oh, no; Pastor. You don't seem to know how damaged I am!'*

Well, you are not alone!

Considerably too, each of the great Biblical saints used of God with a few exceptions – were a damaged cargo. Browse through the cast:

Father Abraham, the idolater and compulsive liar.

Prophet Moses, the #1 wanted murderer.

Lady Rahab, the harlotry success of Jericho City.

King David, the impressive adulterer.

Sister Mary, the bewitching sex trader of Magdala city.

The Saint "Doubting" Thomas; and,

The Very Right Reverend Saint Paul, the hired assassin.

The list could be endless.

One thing strikes the mind though: our backgrounds have a lot to tell on our personality, ability, psyche and comportment. **Somehow, our *roots* bear witness to our *fruits*.** Without doubt, our *roots* become the major variable that determines our altitude in destiny. If we would therefore arrest and correct our defective *roots* with God's help, we would be amazed at how those same *defects* could translate to be *effects*, our weaknesses miraculously turned into strengths.

Take Responsibility; Take Initiative, Stop the *blame game*

Sample the negative impacts and damages – psychological, emotional and fiscal today's *yob* culture in the Western world has left in its trail despite governmental efforts to alleviate this wasting generation of the hopeless and the ill-informed! My advice would be: travel out of your peripheral sphere of influence, into a lesser-advantaged part of the world; you're likely to return home, a changed, rightly informed person, grateful for what Mother England has done for you since birth!

A larger percentage of young adults growing up in Sub-Saharan Africa – including the *10°/40°window* of the world – blame their mid-life troubles on their *birth-grounds*.

'If only I were born in America' they mused, *'things would have been much better.'*

In a quick twist, the Brotherhood in the Diaspora strongly wished they had been born free, in the native lands of their fore-fathers'!

You know what? You could have been born in a garage and this would not have made *you* any lesser a perfect human being! Baby Jesus had been born in a stinking, dirty manger in Bethlehem; yet He'd risen from the grave to be the Lord of all!

Rather than keep passing the buck; you take responsibility for your destiny. The Creator deposited richly in Man, giftings and talents He saw befitted them most, before allowing them to depart the shores of eternity. Initiate positive moves that will better your lot rather than keep holding life's uncontrollable variables responsible for *your* misfortunes. Stop the *blame game.*

> *"And your ancient ruins shall be rebuilt; you shall raise up the foundations of [buildings that have laid waste for] many generations; and you shall be called the Repairer of the Breach, Restorer of streets to Dwell In."*

> ISAIAH 58:12

Chapter 2

Gideon's *Defective* Background

"If the foundations be destroyed, what can the righteous do?"

- KING DAVID

I have attempted to convince you that it is not criminal to possess a disadvantaged or indeed, a defective background. Again, this is no fault of your own. I have also shared with you the inevitability of your background being discovered upon you – particularly if it is your aim and game to cover it up in denials or lies!

I am going to tell you a more compelling reason why you need to get into gears, ready to combat your *defective* background. But before I do, let us delve into Gideon's background.

Whenever the phrase "someone's background" has been used, tell-it-all questionnaires usually have served as accurate determinants to help ascertain the sumtotal of the subject in consideration. Questions such as: *"Where was their origin? What sort of family background did they grow in? What sort of national pride did they have? What job did they – and/or their parents do for a living?" etcetera* would be asked!

Fact-finding about Gideon's background can never be divorced away from the story of the emancipation of Israeli slaves from the harsh bondage in Egypt! This was the background of Gideon's fore-fathers: they were emancipated slaves after 430 years of Egyptian captivity. The *Magna Carta* charter of their freedom read:

> *"I am the LORD thy God, which brought thee out of the land of Egypt, out of the house of bondage.*
>
> *Thou shalt have no other gods before me.*
>
> *Thou shalt not make unto thee any graven image, or any likeness of anything that is in heaven above, or that is in the earth beneath, or that is in the water under the earth:*
>
> *Thou shall not bow down thyself to them, nor serve them: for I the LORD thy God am a jealous God, visiting the iniquity of the fathers upon the children unto the third and fourth generation of them that hate me;*
>
> *And showing mercy unto thousands of them that love, and keep my commandments."*

EXODUS 20:2-6

Notice, the great God – Who orchestrated their emancipation – revealed Himself as a jealous God Who would readily unto the third or fourth generation requite the iniquities of fore-fathers on their generations; because they hated – and provoked Him to jealousy!

This godly jealousy is just the same kind of mutual jealousy rooted in love and aimed at guarding from corrupting influence(s) a husband and a wife display in protective affection toward each other. But Gideon's fore-fathers flaunted God's love. They went awhoring! And as long as they despised God, they remained under tributes to weaker nations.

So we see that Gideon grew up in an idolatrous family, in a young nation that was housed in settlements' tents, in the Land of Promise.

These *new settlers* possessed no national pride. Gideon's generation was at a low ebb; a period of time it was subjected to being constantly raided by the rampaging Midianites and Amalekites, in punitive measures for their idolatry. Gideon's people made their homes in dens, rocks' caves and strongholds!

Their predominant occupation was peasant farming: they tilled, hard, the fertile lands. Despite their hard work, they lived from hand to mouth. They lived in constant fear of enjoying their freedom in the open, free from the harassments of their tormentors. Coupled with all these hardships, they deserted God for *lame* idols!

The background of the 'new Israelite' was that of evil

perpetuation, a cycle of disobedience, lasciviousness and idolatry. Every Israeli child found himself or herself born into it!

Gideon – like his peers – found himself born into his parents' – and fore parents' sinful lifestyles!

One major compelling reason why you'd need to be bold enough to recognize and radically challenge your rotting *roots* is the need to foresee, potentially, a couple of results, emerging. One, your *leaves* – those are your natural reactions to occurrences, later in adulthood – that will bear undeniable signs of corresponding deficiencies resulting from many years of abuse, rejection and suppressed sins. Second, your unhealthy *roots* that will also bear a direct impact of stuntedness and malignity upon your *fruits* – if you manage to bear any!

The Bible teaches:

> *"He that covereth his sins shall not prosper, but whoso confesseth and forsaketh them shall have mercy."*

PROVERBS 28:13

The first grade troubles in any man's life have been discovered to have been inherited. For example, Jacob's craftiness was learned by him from his own mother Rebecca. We see how parents, indeed, can affect their children's destinies. Problem is, inherited problems, if not quickly arrested could translate into stigmatized curses, thus setting up a chain reaction whereby an abused person at youth becomes an abuser or possibly a predator in adulthood.

Jabez was being cursed from the womb that nurtured him while he was just a sinless, helpless fetus. When he came out of the womb, a ready, steady curse awaited him. He became accursed instantaneously!

The unpleasant conditions associated with Jabez's gestation made his mom *feel* she had to retaliate on the sinless little creature. His father may have abandoned the mother upon learning that she was in a state of expectancy; I may not tell. She may have been dated raped, we weren't told. What is apparent is that the mother misused her power of attorney or authority over her child. This is why I implore parents – mothers and fathers or guardians – in the name of the LORD, not to speak a negative word against the destiny of any of their children! If you however fail to heed my warning and rather choose to curse your children, that's fine, *just* by you. I'd step the challenge up a notch further, inviting such *troubled* children to "come out"; come to the place of the Cross, where Emmanuel's blood flows! You come with anticipation, ready to take a *Blood-bath*!

Oh, I am aware there are horrible parents who themselves had had a horrible childhood or upbringing. But thank God for the cleansing and atoning curse-removing power of the Blood of Jesus Christ. Jabez broke loose from under his mother's evil spell by calling on the name of the Lord. [1]

Does anyone identify with Jabez?

You too will break loose from those curses of negative words spoken against you, the spirit of negativism, the abuse and the neglect through the power in the Blood of the Lamb. Scripture teaches we overcame him (the devil and his evil works) by the blood of the Lamb, and by the word of our testimony. [2]

According to the story of the man born blind whom Jesus personally encountered – and reported upon, we notice that apart from one's *very own* sins, inherited consequences of sins committed by our progenitors could be borne by our generation if we would choose to be God-haters! [3] But this particular man met the Savior: he was healed at that encounter; it was his day!

The Particular Evil of Gideon's Generation

The Bible says:

> *"And the children of Israel did evil in the sight of the LORD: and the LORD delivered them into the hand of Midian seven years."*

> JUDGES 6:1

Their evil practice meant that their disavowed Master delivered them into the hands of the merciless Midianites who spoiled them. Their cycles of disobedience had evoked His holy wrath.

Some of us bear a middle name which however may be silent most times. This fact does not annul the statutory fact that it is *our* name. In the same token, God's 'silent' middle name is called *"Jealous."* A person's name gives meaning to their essence.

> *"For thou shalt worship no other god: for the LORD, whose name is jealous, is a jealous God."*

> EXODUS 34:14

Thus, because of His jealous nature and essence, He commanded them:

> *"Thou shalt have no other gods before me.*

> EXODUS 20:3

The children of Israel continued to eschew God's basic warning, unabated! Through Judges 2:10–19, we read of their summary character as a lawless, reckless generation of human beings. The Word bore witness against them that:

> *"In those days there was no king in Israel: every man did that which was right in his own eyes."*

> JUDGES 21:25

God had specifically, long fore-warned them through the mouth of Moses His Prophet: *"Ye shall not do after all the things that we do here this day, every man whatsoever is right in his own eyes."* [4] Unfortunately, they would trail the path dishonoring to God; they would choose lawlessness!

The Problem inherent in Lawlessness

Once lawlessness is granted domain, for example, in a family; it rapidly perpetuates itself in a vicious circle of mandated hardship, pains, aches and sorrows. Every member of such a home will not know *any* peace until the root-cause has been exhumed.

In the same vein, when a leader errs, whilst the throne may be at relative peace, the subjects however, would pay dearly for such leader's errors. An instance of this was demonstrated when David had slighted God's counsel – and in presumption, had taken a census of the Israelites.

> *"And again the anger of the LORD was kindled against Israel, and he moved David against them to say, Go, number Israel and Judah."*

2 SAMUEL 24:1

For this iniquity which David had eventually publicly repented of in the tenth verse of that passage; God, through the mouth of Prophet Gad had given the king, three conditions of punishment, one of which *had* to be implemented.

> *"So Gad came to David, and told him, and said unto him, Shall seven years of famine come unto thee in thy land? or wilt thou flee three months before thine enemies, while they pursue thee? or that there be three days' pestilence in thy land? now advise, and see what answer I shall return to him that sent me."*

2 SAMUEL 24:13

Notice, none of those penalties would convey a direct sentence upon King David's life but the Kingdom.

This is a chilling truth! Seven years of famine will wreck havoc in the city but will not leave the king's dining tables without a constant daily supply of dainty meats. Similarly, if the enemy forces swooped in on the land, David's soldiers would smart for it: the anointed king had in the past escaped seemingly inescapable tight sieges. This is the main reason God asks us to pray for our anointed leaders. He knows the subjects would pay dearly for a leader's misdeeds.

We read in 1 TIMOTHY 2:1–2:

> *"I exhort therefore, that, first of all, supplications, prayers, intercessions, and giving of thanks, be made for all men;*
>
> *For kings, and for all that are in authority: that we may lead a quiet and peaceable life in all godliness and honesty."*

David ran into God's arms and threw himself at Him the way a silly toddler nestles in his father's embrace. Father God was eventually moved to pronounce – on him – the least sentence of the three; albeit of drastic consequences, even for the duration of a few hours:

> *"So the LORD sent a pestilence upon Israel from the morning even to the time appointed: and there died of the people from Dan even to Beersheba seventy thousand men."*

2 SAMUEL 24:15

Just imagine 70 000 souls snuffed out like candles in the wind! That was before God nodded 'enough' to the angel of death. "That seemed a huge ransom to pay for setting light God's counsel against taking just a mere census," we would say. God would say: "David's act was reckless!"

The problem inherent in lawlessness is recklessness. Lawlessness is the disregard of the law – whether slightly, partially or absolutely! Therefore, a lawless people are often a reckless people.

Now, reckless individuals have a major ill. That illness is called insensitivity. You may call it callousness. Some other person may name it selfishness. Insensitivity, callousness or selfishness is like the deaf ordered to march to the drumbeat of a drummer. Insensitivity is like comparing side by side, a partially sighted, to a person a with a *20-20 vision.*

Early Signs of Recklessness

A reckless father scolds the growing young adult *anyhow, anywhere.* A reckless wife neglects her immediate home, husband and children for a third party; mainly her close relatives – and probably her closest friends. A reckless friend disregards the healthy boundaries or checks set within a relationship, partnership or friendship. A reckless husband shows early signs of recklessness by not providing for his home's basic spiritual cover, material needs and emotional dispensations.

Furthermore, reckless people are devoid of others' feelings. They are often a selfish, pitiable people. They, more than seldom, tend to prefer things of ethereal values – like gratifying dietary, physical or sensual desires, laudable achievements or ambitions – to the sublime, eternal values.

Balaam had both his eyes fixed upon the *"wages of unrighteousness"* as well as executing an unrighteous ministry! [5] A lady mortgaged her fiancé's future *absolute* trust in her so cheaply by allowing him passage rights before marriage. A student cheated in the examination – and is yet proud of his certificate. An intending migrant destroyed their passport and related documents which they have – under oath – sworn as lost; yet gained citizenship without blinking an eye! Another, a rightful citizen, bartered citizenship in an arranged, shambolic wedding. The *workaholic* father compensated his children's hollowing emotions with a brief ride in the top-of-the-range, open-roof *BMW sports*. The businessman/woman went in pursuit of multi-million pound contract to the capital city – and that, at the expense of a midweek church service or personal fellowship with God, not a mistaken once, nor twice; this has become their *mammon-nary* habit.

You see, the Bible refers to reckless, lawless people as *"past feeling."* [6] The Apostle Paul in his letter to Bishop Timothy likens insensitive people to lepers. Sufferers' hearts, he says, are *"seared with a hot iron."* [7]

Two Examples of Recklessness: Jonathan and Governor Felix

Jonathan, Saul's son

Jonathan – like his father King Saul – was an epitome of recklessness.

Reckless people – like those dare devil drivers captured on *Police Videos* – approach destructions and yet continue headlong, daring the consequences. They always endeavor to take along with them to the grave, some innocent soul(s). Jonathan would *willy-nilly* accompany his distressed father on that journey to destruction in spite of his knowledge of the perfect will of God for his life, David and the Kingdom. He had become an emotional weakling paralyzed by his affection towards his dad. The insensitivity venom had reached his heart.

How many homes have been ruined by a spouse's unbroken affection toward their biological parents and/or siblings?

Some mothers, adept at spiritual wickedness still have their children's birth cords wrapped round their apron strings. They manipulate such helpless children, at will! They are adept at manipulating their children. Look, your misdemeanor is nothing short of witchcraft. People like yourself have ruined – and still continue to ruin countless marriages and lives!

Robert Liardon once said: *"There is nothing more dangerous than getting to the middle of the road and not knowing what next to do."* How true that was of Jonathan – and probably many of us?

Jonathan could not deny that God gave him a firsthand foreknowledge of the state of affairs of the Kingdom of Israel; yet he could not convert that revelation knowledge to his advantage and safe-keep. What a waste!

What good to any is 'revealed' knowledge that is unimplemented?

In 1 SAMUEL 23:16–17 we were told:

> *"And Jonathan Saul's son arose, and went to David into the wood, and strengthened his hand in God.*
>
> *And he said unto him, Fear not: for the hand of Saul my father shall not find thee; and thou shalt be king over Israel, **and I shall be next unto thee;** and that also Saul my father knoweth."*
>
> (EMPHASIS; MINE.)

Jonathan perished unduly.

May you receive the grace to be able to implement and incorporate *revealed* knowledge into your earthly doings that you may be preserved. The difference between the foolish and wise is the implementation of *revealed* knowledge on all issues that stare them both, in the face.

Didn't the Lord promise that the foundation and success of His Church against the gates of hell would be 'revealed' knowledge? [8]

Governor Felix

Governor Felix's name had every chance to secure a

space in the Lamb's Book of Life but for his corrupt, bribe-ridden, insensitive mind. He lost his eternity.

Earlier, his wife Drusilla, a Jewess had been impressing upon his heart, the way of the Lord. What a fine witness!

Drusilla exhibits God's expectation of saved wives of the unregenerate high and the nobles, to apply *womanly affection* and yet a holy pressure upon their husbands' tender hearts, to woo them to the living faith in Christ.

Mrs. Drusilla Felix turned the full-steam on her husband, now, that she caught wind of a rumor that the fiery Apostle Paul was within reach, though bound in chains. She ensured that Felix met Apostle Paul. We read of their encounter with the Apostle in Acts 24:24–25:

> *"And after certain days, when Felix came with his wife Drusilla, which was a Jewess, he sent for Paul, and heard him concerning the faith in Christ.*
>
> *And as he reasoned of righteousness, temperance, and judgment to come, Felix trembled, and answered, Go thy way for this time; when I have a convenient season, I will call for thee."*

We see Governor Felix's depraved little heart in the next verse:

> *"He hoped also that money should have been given him of Paul, that he might loose him; wherefore he sent for him the oftener, and communed with him."*

Of course, Apostle Paul would not give Felix a bribe. He was on course for a higher calling. He had met with the shamefaced, corrupt Governor – and had witnessed about the Lord to him. He had done the part Heaven had assigned him. Now he was *en route* to Emperor Nero's Rome where he would ultimately fulfill Jesus' prophecy:

> *"And ye shall be brought before governors and kings for my name sake, for a testimony against them and the Gentiles."*

MATTHEW 10:18

Paul esteemed higher, the eternal value of the kings and the nobles hearing his witness unto them of the name of Christ more than his own personal freedom. He bore the vision seed of the Heavenly Kingdom in his heart, those prison chains notwithstanding.

Felix, in contrast, fixed his gaze on mere *ethereal* blessings. The governor had eyes for bribe, material-ism, fame, position – and power that money can bring.

Paul saw the chains as a promotion to the cause of the Gospel; Felix saw them as an intentional punitive meas-ure aimed at dampening the Apostle's high morale.

So, guess what he did?

He therefore *"left Paul bound"* in chains as a prisoner, for the next couple of years. [9]

What a pitiable Governor Felix! His heart had been captured by vain gold.

Just before you start shaking your head at poor Felix; you ought to ask: *'How many other Felix's are out there whose hearts have been captured not only by gold but by vain girls or vain glories?'*

Is your heart a captive of ethereal or eternal stuff?

If They Repent

Peradventure the reckless repents; they must be jealously, closely monitored for fears of possible backsliding. The reason the Israel of Gideon's day did relapse into sin ever so often was because there was no king in the land. In those times, an earthly king served as an enforcer of Heaven's mandate on the earth. The apostles of Christ were given grace *"to promote obedience to the faith ... among all nations."* [10]

'Oh, that excludes me since I am not an apostle,' you seem to say!

But wait. If you are a Blood-bought, born-again christian, Heaven recognizes you as Her Ambassador! Ambassadors represent their home governments to foreign lands where they have been designated to serve.

Friend, Heaven recognizes you as Her ambassador to planet earth:

> *"Now then we are ambassadors for Christ ..."*
>
> 2 CORINTHIANS 5:20

Apart from representing home interests to the for-eign country, embassy and their staff perform other varied duties, one of which is their uncommon ability to 'keep track' of their citizens' whereabouts and well-being upon entry into that particular terri-tory, if they have registered with the embassy.

In like manner, God will demand of the Christian ambassador an accurate accounting of the new converts' whereabouts and well-being – spiritual, emotional and financial – who have been entrusted unto their care. [11]

More committal efforts will be required from the matured Christian worker, if their converts have come to *the faith* from a backlog of brokenness, affliction, humiliation or rejection. These – and many more – are examples of ensnared backgrounds or *defective roots* I have been discussing! Thus, a Christian worker, in order to become an effective and successful discipler of souls from such historical backgrounds must possess plenty of patience, grace, wit and wisdom. More, they should not work alone! In His wisdom, God made it easier for us by creating opportunities of fellowship with other believers. In Hebrews 10:24–25, we are encouraged thus:

> *"And let us consider one another to provoke unto love and to good works:*
>
> *Not forsaking the assembling of ourselves together, as the manner of some is; but exhorting one another: and so much the more as ye see the day approaching."*

In various portions of Acts 2, we find the secret of spiritual sustenance of the Early Church:

> *"And they continued steadfastly in the apostles' doctrine and fellowship, and in breaking of bread, and in prayers."*

The key word here is *"fellowship"* which can be further translated as: *"Togetherness." "Tenacity." "Closeness."* It is in our steadfast continuance in the teachings of scriptures and fellowship; *our* togetherness, *our* tenacity and closeness lay our sustenance strength in the spiritual walk. In fellowshipping *and* sharing with the brethren, our communal as well as personal securities are guaranteed as Christ's Bride.

Most of us have seen the documentary films on African wildlife on the *Discovery Channel*. You've seen that the predator, for example, a lion, is only stealthily targeting just one stray, forgetful, un-herded, laid-back, unwatchful member of the herd. Its other target may just be the complacent one, just a little separated from the whole herd by mere petti-ness, 'puffiness' or pride. No predator ever aims at a random catch from the herd: its choices for a surprise attack can only fit the descriptions earlier mentioned. This is why we are strongly admonished:

> *"Be sober, be vigilant; because your adversary the devil as a roaring lion, walketh about, seeking whom he may devour:*

Whom resist steadfast in the faith, knowing that the same afflictions are accomplished in your brethren that are in the world."

1 PETER 5: 8–9

How do we resist the devil?

We resist the devil by being steadfast in the faith.

We become grounded in our faith when we read and meditate upon the Word of God, day and night! Soon, in meditation, we begin to exchange our former mindset with a renewed mind of Christ. Our thought-life and perspective to life in general begin to be umpired and undergirded by the Word of God – and His Holy Spirit! Mandatorily, our thought, speech and behavioral patterns follow suit. We crave for more intimacy with Him, His Word and fellowship *with* His other children. We share together, often drawing parallels in our dealings with the Lord – and indeed, in His dealings *with* us!

The secret to a christian's consistency is found in Acts 2:44:

> *"And all that believed were together."*

By maintaining a close sense of togetherness with like-minded folk, the christians in the early church were endued with strength from within – same available strength, a large proportion of today's christians lack! This closely-knit framework of strength-formation made it impossible for the devil and his host to penetrate their circle; little wonder, their quality of character was ensured!

> *"And they, continuing daily with one accord in the temple and breaking bread from house to house did eat their meat with gladness and singleness of heart."*

ACTS 2:46

The outcome of their daily *'communion'* was obvious. It was characteristically, a supernatural growth.

> *"And the Lord added to the church daily such as should be saved."*

ACTS 2:47

There is an inherent danger, I have observed over the years, which a child of God is prone to fall into when – for seemingly more plausible reasons to his/her senses – he/she breaks fellowship either with God or other believers. He/she stands a robust chance of being devoured by the devourer. Ostracizing their intended victim from help sources had always been the most effective tool of spiritist attacks. Therefore, if a believer brakes fellowship and by divine intervention manages to escape the devil's stranglehold; his life's chart will at best resemble a merging together of contorted, loopy *u's* and *n's*. Thus, if *fellowship absenteeism* is the major struggle you are experiencing in your spiritual walk, doubtlessly, you occupy a dangerous territory.

May you receive such an awesome grace today that will enable you effect a positive change so as to secure, enhance and fulfill your destiny in life – and in the Kingdom of your Father.

A Summary of Gideon's Generational Background

Because of the evil they and their fore fathers per-petuated, the children of Israel walloped in great afflictions and miseries.

This summary – evident in Judges 6:1-6 – described their state of affairs:

- They were idolatrous;
- The Lord delivered them unto afflicters who came in swarms and wasted them;
- They developed a sense of fear, shame and defeat; and thus began to hide in dens and caves – a kind of 'inferiority complex' ; and finally,
- They were greatly impoverished – until they deemed it fit to cry unto the Lord, their Deliverer.

Chapter 3

God's Two Main Agents of Deliverance

"If one advances confidently in the direction of his dreams, and endeavors to live the life which he has imagined, he will meet with a success unexpected in uncommon hours."

- HENRY DAVID THOREAU

We have seen the damage done by the enemies of the Lord to the chosen of Jehovah who lapsed into their generation's sinful traditions. We also have read of their eventual response to this assault of the devil because they cried unto the Lord. [1]

Quite understandably, not until we are fed up with our predicaments and have lifted up our eyes toward the Lord of hosts for deliverance would He avail Himself unto us.

Let me cite a few examples.

Not until Israel cried unto the Lord in Egypt did the Lord God rouse Himself and react favorably to their plight. We read that *"God looked upon the children of Israel, and ... had respect unto them."* [2] Similarly, Jabez cried unto the Lord against the curse his mother had placed upon him before the effects of that evil pronouncement were reversed: *"And Jabez called on the God of Israel ... And God granted him that which he requested."* [3] Blind Bartimaeus was fed up being a highway side beggar. He spared not his lungs despite mob opposition! He cried: *"Jesus, thou son of David, have mercy on me."* [4] *"Immediately,"* the Bible says, *"he received his sight and followed Jesus in the way."* [5]

Father God longs to hear us call out unto Him in our troubles and afflictions. He confirmed through the mouth of Prophet Jeremiah:

> *"Call unto me, and I will answer thee, and shew thee great and mighty things, which thou knowest not."*

> JEREMIAH 33: 3

Couple Your Cry with a High Expectation

Not only must we cry to God for deliverance and help, our cries must be attended with a high expectation that He hears – and will answer us!

"And this is the confidence that we have in him, that, if we ask anything according to his will, he heareth us."

1 JOHN 5:14

All through the scriptures, miracles happened only when men were high in expectation of what God can – and *will* do! Expectation gives birth to manifestation.

God responds to His children's cries ever so often in two concise ways: through sending His prophets and His holy angels!

The emancipation of Gideon – and the Israelites from the wasteful, attacking raids of the Ishmaelites wasn't going to be an exception.

In the following few pages, I shall attempt to discuss succinctly, God's two main agents of deliverance.

First, the prophet sent.

"And Israel was greatly impoverished because of the Midianites and the children of Israel cried unto the LORD.

And it came to pass, when the children of Israel cried unto the Lord because of the Midianites,

That the LORD sent a prophet unto the children of Israel …"

JUDGES 6:6–8

Second, the angel dispatched.

> *"And there came an angel of the LORD, and sat under an oak which was in Ophrah, that pertained unto Joash the Abiezrite: and his son Gideon threshed wheat by the winepress, to hide it from the Midianites."*

JUDGES 6:11

God's Two Main Agents of Deliverance: The place of God's Prophet

Without doubt, there is the place of a God sent prophet in your prevailing predicaments if your emancipation must be realized. Do not think you can achieve your feat, dreams and aspirations alone. We read: *"that the Lord sent a prophet to the children of Israel ..."* [6]

So, what then, is the place of the prophet sent?

Clearly stated in Hoshea 11:13, we read of the importance of a prophet of God:

> *"And by a prophet the Lord brought Israel out of Egypt, and by a prophet was he preserved."*

This verse obviously refers to the four hundred and thirty year Israeli bondage in Egypt – and Moses, the deliverer.

This prophecy of long captivity would serve a dual purpose. One, it would serve as a confirmation and an assurance to Abram that he will indeed inherit

Canaan, the land He (God) had just promised him; a promise deemed by Abram as too good to be true. Two, God would use same word of prophecy to serve a judgment on Abram's doubt of His power to make good what He had said!

> *"And he said, Lord GOD, whereby shall I know that I shall inherit it?"*

> *"And he said unto Abram, Know of a surety that thy seed shall be a Stranger in a land that is not theirs, and shall serve them; and they shall afflict them four hundred years."*

GENESIS 15:8; 13

You see, when God trusts us so much, He expects that we wholly trust Him too in return.

Isn't lack of trust the core concern in all relationship breakdowns?

Relationship with God is no exception. The long captivity foretold was God's judgment of Abram's doubt of the Almighty's potency, much as He would later judge Priest Zechariah with dumbness at his doubting of the glad tidings Angel Gabriel had brought him that his wife Elisabeth would bear him their son, John, even in their very ripe old ages! [7]

Two Major Tasks of a Prophet

Back to Hoshea 11:13, we notice two major tasks of a prophet as set forth:

- For deliverance and;
- Preservation.

These are the two major tasks of an anointed prophet to a person, people, generation or place. God's orderly framework of running His entire creation forbids Him performing *all* of the tasks. In other words, there is the *division of labor* principle in God's corporate entity. *Take for instance; man must bear the precious seed of the Gospel to his fellow men. Angels, will never preach.* That is why I feel strong empathy for those who despise and write off God's servants based purely on their looks, dresses or vernacular! Friend, beware! That man or woman of God bears the mandate of Father God to ensue your freedom – and not just your freedom from that bondage and affliction, but your preservation also.

In 2 Chronicles 20:20, we are commanded to believe God's true servants:

> *"Believe in the Lord your God, so shall ye be established, believe His prophets, so shall ye prosper."*

Your prosperity is ensured by the ministry of God's prophet sent to you. But you must believe him and accept God's message on his lips.

After miraculously experiencing deliverance from a gruesome armed-robbery attack where my first car, belongings, cash and documents were robbed at gunpoint at an entry point into the ancient city of Ibadan, Nigeria, April 11th, 1996; the Lord directed me to proceed to the southwest part of the city. I was on His mandate to plant a new church. The money I depended upon for paying the hall rent for the first three months had been in my brown leather briefcase in the car!

A month later, while I surveyed on foot, Challenge area - a commercial part of the ancient African city - for a probable location of a new Church and souls to start with, I was led of the Holy Spirit into a small barbing salon primarily, to share the Words of life. I met about seven young men in there aged between 23 and 30 years. After about twenty minutes of preaching, I made an altar call for anybody who would want to surrender their life to Christ. No one responded. Nevertheless, I shared the grace and started for the door.

Almost immediately, a young man doubled his pace after mine, and once outside the salon, asked for my excuse. He asked me back – and led me into the adjacent storage room. It was a hot, disheveled, cob-web ridden smaller room. In here, this young man poured out his heart. His friends out in the main lobby laughed hysterically. They said he had a lily liver. But this man required an urgent financial intervention to revamp his ailing business. He was an avowed moslem who confessed that he had enough 'belief' that I was sent of God to him as I'd preached exactly on many issues of his life!

I knew I had only spoken the words of the Lord as He gave me utterance; I wouldn't know I had touched on *any* issue that pertained specifically to anyone. I had enough pressing *issues* of my own! But I was overwhelmed with compassion for him!

In that dinghy, shabby, claustrophobia-causing storeroom space, he knelt down and I poured the anointing oil on him asking the Lord to seal his requests.

A month and a half later, I'd passed by his premises again, on visitation. This man reported that two weeks earlier, he'd miraculously received more than N85 000 worth of materials that revamped his business. (That was a lot of money that would build you a comfortable self-built bungalow, in those days.) He'd invested the cash inflow into his business, but also furthered his building project that had being stampeded for sometime. This young man earnestly besought us to start our church's weekly services from his seventy-two square foot salon.

There, on Sunday August 18, 1996; in that small space, our church history began! [8]

This is the point I am making: your job it is to locate *your* prophet, whatever the costs! Bear in mind, that the issue of spiritual fathership/sonship is not restricted by physical or geographic borders! This prophet alone carries that preservation balm you'd need – not for just one victory, but multiple victories. This is *your* preserving prophet! As salt acts as a preservative, this prophet sent by God exercises a seasoning effect on your life for *your* prolonged fruitfulness and sweatless triumphs.

In 2 Kings 13, we read a story of the Israelites who

provoked God to wrath through idolatry. As recompense, God's people were ensnared and wasted by two generations of Hazael the King of Syria and Benhadad his son. The oppressions by the enemies lasted until God's people repented and besought Him.

In quick response to their cries *"the Lord gave Israel a saviour"* who ensured their deliverance and peaceful restoration.

> *"And Jehoahaz besought the LORD, and the LORD hearkened unto him: for he saw the oppression of Israel, because the King of Syria oppressed them.*
>
> *And the LORD gave Israel a saviour, so that they went out from under the hand of the Syrians: and the children of Israel dwelt in their tents, as before time."*
>
> 2 Kings 13:4–5

Do you know who that *savior* was? It was the *distinctive* Prophet Elisha.

Recognize Your Mentor and the Appropriate Actions to Take towards Him

Soon, Israel was besieged again by the Syrian wasters! King Joash of Israel needed not waste time. He knew too well his place of preservation. He recognized the importance of the ministry of the prophet, his *savior*.

Now, Prophet Elisha was on his death bed, old and

stricken in years. Watch this mystery that always surrounds a true prophet: though old and inactive, his office would never age. He may be long-gone, but his words will be long here! [9]

> *"For the LORD thy God hath chosen him out of all thy tribes, to stand to minister in the name of the LORD, him and his sons for ever."*
>
> DEUTERONOMY 18:5

The victorious Church of Jesus Christ is *"built upon the foundation of the apostles and the prophets, Jesus Christ himself being the chief corner stone."* [10] This is the reason the Church is eternally triumphant. [11]

King Joash not only knew *where* to run to, he knew *what* – appropriate thing – to do. He did not despise Elisha's weariness on the deathbed. How often a protégé needs take heed *not* to despise their mentor's defenselessness in weakness – or indeed, children, their parents! We must not seize the opportunity to get even with God's anointed even if such opportunity avails itself. Doing so will be like stirring into motion, a gigantic tide of a self-destroying prophecy!

What appropriate thing did King Joash do on arriving at Elisha's deathbed?

In 2 Kings 13:14 we read:

> *"And Joash the king of Israel came down unto him, and wept over his face, and said, O my father; my father, the chariot of Israel, and the horsemen thereof."*

Let me amplify this verse above in simple practicable pieces of instructions, aimed at giving you guidelines as to what appropriate actions you'd potentially need to take towards your mentor.

First, we read: *"Joash the king came down unto him."*

Could that translate Joash prepared to humble his heart before the prophet of God?

Very much so!

Second, not only did he prepare to humble his heart; the king honored the prophet by *coming down to him, bodily, at his death-bed.*

King Joash could have sent just an ordinary servant to the prophet as rich but leprous Naaman did to Elisha; but no! [12] He knew better. He knew doing that would amount to dishonoring the anointed.

If you live in close proximity to your mentor, for example, meeting him physically and presenting your *issues* would be more advantageous than sending him a text.

Third, *love on your prophet.*

More than just gracing the bedside of the dying prophet, King Joash hugged the anointed man of God!

In other words, the king *loved on* Elisha.

You too can love on your mentor in many other ways more than a mere physical presence or a hug. Spend your time praying for him – and his family! Protect their secrets if you're privileged in the know. Sow financial seeds into their lives and ministry! These are some ways you *love on* your mentor!

We notice the resulting sequence of events once respect, love and honor had been bestowed upon whom it was due: the anointing for the distressed king's deliverance from his oppressors was released. His preservation was ensured. In a melodramatic turn of events, victory was ensured not on the battle-field, but just by the humble king believing in and bestowing honor upon *his* prophet.

Victory was ensured in the spiritual realm using the prophet of God as a divine connection with God. True lasting victories are often decided this way.

Fourth, *obey the words of God through his mouth.*

We see Elisha issuing out commands to the dis-tressed king. They were very simple commands!

> *"And Elisha said unto him, Take bow and arrows. And he took unto him bow and arrows.*
>
> *And he said to the king of Israel, Put thine hand upon the bow. And he put his hand, upon it: and Elisha put his hands upon the king's hands.*
>
> *And he said, Open the window eastward. And he opened it. Then Elisha said, Shoot. And he shot. And he said, The arrow of the LORD's deliverance, and the arrow of deliverance from Syria ...*

And he said, Take the arrows. And he took them. And he said unto the king of Israel, Smite upon the ground. And he smote thrice, and stayed.

And the man of God was wroth with him, and said, Thou shouldest have smitten five or six times; then hadst thou smitten Syria till thou hadst consumed it: whereas now thou shalt smite Syria but thrice."

2 KINGS 13:15–19

Fifth, *allow your mentor's hands to couple yours.*

In this story, one dramatic event stands out and is worthy of our notice. We read that *"Elisha put his hands upon the king's hands."* [13] In other words, the prophet of God coupled his anointed hands with the king's shaking hands. Elisha's hands were supposedly meant to be weak, frail hands; yet they were the winning hands of God.

When the Israelites fought against the wild Amalekites, Moses the prophet of God was up on the mount with his arms raised to Heaven in intercession. The Bible records that his arms were heavy and weary. At the brief moment he rested his arms, the Amalekites recorded brief winning. When this was noticed, Moses asked Hur and Aaron to help support his arms while Joshua fought below in the valley. Moses' supported arms proved to be the only winning factor that day! [14]

This mystery about the hands of your mentor in yours, his arms raised on your behalf to Heaven is what you must ensure in order that you may repeatedly record many an outstanding good success in your life's calling.

Some business people in the church shy back from engaging the anointing of the anointed in their businesses. They conceal profits and do not generally pay their tithe. You deceive no one else but your very self. The truth is that that way is the guaranteed way of you bringing in little and earning into a bag with holes. Make no mistake about the issue; the hands of God's chosen prophet must couple yours to ensure you have repeated success!

Do you know the prophet whose hands had always coupled each American President's for the past four decades?

Would you remember whom Mr. George W. Bush was last sighted with in a Church service barely 24 hours before the crucial, neck-in-neck November 7, 2000 U.S Elections? That prophet was just a word short of endorsing the then Texas Governor Bush at that service that day.

It was none other than the Reverend Dr. Billy Graham.

There is no magic wand to it; it is God's mystery in working the supernatural. If it worked for President George W. Bush, it will work for you.

Come to think of it. How could a true child of God venture out into the open wide world filled with all the caprices of the devil, without the hands of his Shepherd fully coupled with his? How could you attempt to cleanly win a contract or get engaged to a spouse without your Pastor's hands standing with yours in total agreement?

Such naive immature souls have always ended up pawns in the devil's tight grips – or their precious time could have been spent delayed or frustrated in fruitless endeavors.

Allowing the hands of your prophet to couple yours also extends unto supporting or partnering with him in his God-called vision.

Summarily, therefore, five practicable things will ensure your deliverance, establishment and preservation:

- Locate the prophet sent to you.
- Respect, honor and love on your mentor.
- Obey his instructions without questioning.
- Ensure your prophet's hands couple yours before you venture out into the open.
- Always lift the prophet's weary hands up at all cost. Partner – financially, prayerfully and otherwise – with him and share his God-given visions.

Who then is a true prophet?

In Deuteronomy 18:21–22, we find the answer:

"And if thou say in thine heart, How shall we know the word which the LORD hath not spoken?

When a prophet speaketh in the name of the LORD, if the thing follow not, nor come to pass,

*that is the thing which the LORD hath not spoken,
but the prophet hath spoken it presumptuously:
thou shalt not be afraid of him."*

This is the basic acid test; *the validation test* a true prophet of God must be subjected to. I do not particularly think the richness of the color of his robe, miter, *clerical-collar*; three-piece suit or haircut style is of primary relevance here. Rather, the question we must ask is: *Is this a man or woman worthy to have destinies entrusted with?*

Also, we are not just talking of *"baby prophets"* whose words appear like comets for a little while before disappearing into dark oblivion! Rather, any occupying a prophetic-office must be tested, proven and validated. The validation of any prophet is inherent in the ability of his prophecies being actualized – even over a long period of time.

Child Samuel, three, was a prophet whose word wasn't to be shoved aside – even at that tender age! He'd prophesied the cessation of Prophet Eli's lineage from being priests unto the Lord! It took a little over one hundred and twenty years before the fulfillment of that prophecy. Abiathar, the only surviving serving priest from Eli's descendants along with Adonijah and General Joab were soon implicated in a mutiny against the new administration of King Solomon. This earned Abiathar a summary expulsion from the priestly office. His dismissal order was issued in 1 Kings 2:26–27:

"And unto Abiathar the priest said the king, Get thee to Anathoth, unto thine own fields; for thou art worthy of death: but I will not at this time put thee to death, because thou barest the ark of the Lord GOD before David my father, and because thou hast been afflicted in all wherein my father was afflicted.

So Solomon thrust out Abiathar from being priest unto the LORD; that he might fulfil the word of the LORD, which he spake concerning the house of Eli in Shiloh."

Of the six people whose names were foretold in the entire scriptures before their birth, little King Josiah would be one! The *"man of God"* from Judah – who had prophesied Josiah's birth and name – had traveled to Bethel and prophesied against Jeroboam. The reason for that cry against the king was as a result of his despicable idolatry and his motive of competing with Jerusalem as the sole center of worship. This same *"man of God"* had prophesied Josiah's revolutionary reforms in Judah. But it would take a little over three hundred years for his prophecy to come to pass. [15]

Furthermore, two questions ought to be asked to ascertain the truthfulness of a prophet:

- Is his life consistent with that of Christ and the teachings enunciated in the Holy Scriptures?
- Is he compassionate with the anointing?

These are questions about the fruits of a tree and the

tree itself. Hear the Lord say it most clearly in Matthew 7:18–20:

> *"A good tree cannot bring forth evil fruit, neither can a corrupt tree bring forth good fruit.*
>
> *Every tree that bringeth not forth good fruit is hewn down, and cast into the fire.*
>
> *Wherefore by their fruits ye shall know them."*

If any prophet lives or encourages people to live away from the dictates of Christ, we must eschew him even if his words have successfully passed the *validation test*. Hear Moses' counsel:

> *"If there arise among you a prophet, or a dreamer of dreams, and giveth thee a sign or a wonder,*
>
> *And the sign or the wonder come to pass, whereof he spake unto thee, saying, Let us go after other gods, which thou hast not known, and let us serve them;*
>
> *Thou shalt not hearken unto the words of that prophet, or that dreamer of dreams: for the LORD your God proveth you, to know whether ye love the LORD your God with all your heart and with all your soul."*

DEUTERONOMY 13:1–3

Do not lust after an anointing ordinarily. The *anointed* must necessarily demonstrate a life-style that is compatible with the anointing they exude.

You would be surprised by the atrocities that permeate the spiritist underworld.

Most African false prophets strap *juju* under their cloaks around the waistband. Some others wear incisions on the upper cleft of their lower lips to help activate their pronouncements – a lower lip they are necessarily mandated to lick to activate a demon-release before each pronouncement!

So now onwards, when you notice a 'lip-licking' prophet, you should quickly be able to recognize their falsity. Jesus says *"by their fruits ye shall know them."* [16]

Sequel to our *first* calling to be followers of Christ, [17] our *second* calling is to become 'fruit inspectors'! [18] We do not just hear the words preached *and* search the scriptures if they be so; we also inspect the tree bearing the fruits. Halleluyah!

Since *covetousness is equated with idolatry;* [19] we may further rightly suspect the falsity of a prophet by inquiring if he/she has just one legally recognized spouse! And if they are not married; are they pure – and *single* in intent?

If they are found to flaunt these 'basics'; they are to be ditched, their great anointing notwithstanding.

Finally, does your chosen prophet curse when provoked?

Find out from their circle of influence if their private life matches their public life.

Are they compassionate and kind?

Do they easily forgive when offended, or do they bear grudges?

Are they a complainer and/or a grumbler?

Are they sensitive to others' feelings and words?

Are they quick to apologize and ask for pardon if in the wrong?

Do they pretend to always be so spiritual, most of the time?

What other reactions of your chosen prophet have you noticed him/her display in their displeased, angry or disappointed moments?

A true servant of God must be controlled, temperamental, compassionate and humane *inspite* of the anointing they carry!

In my learning however, I have personally observed that most prophets just beginning to operate in the prophetic ministry tend to be rash. They always clamored for instant judgment at injustices, much like Elijah had, on those three sets of brigades that had attempted to arrest him on Mount Carmel. Some others may just be as impatient as Peter was with Malchus' ear, and quite a few, probably, as egoistic as Jonah.

With time however, a servant of God ought to grow and mature into their designated office. Thus, it is their unwillingness to outgrow their immaturity that poses them a threat to be labeled as "false" rather than the genuineness of their calling.

I am still growing in the ministry. But quite much earlier, I'd been privileged to meet an elite family with beautiful daughters who eventually got born again and joined our newly planted church. Shortly, the Lord revealed to me that one of the teenaged ladies had "missed the mark." My prophetic background had ignited the evangelist's zeal in me which had undercut my pastoral role!

In a sharp rebuke, I had denounced her; even later, to her parents' face!

You probably could accurately prophesy what events *did* eventually follow.

None of us in life deserves a hard knock on an already aching, throbbing head. Exhortation may not be appropriate in a period comfort is crucially needed. My pastorate lost the entire family of eight; *just like that!*

Bishop David Oyedepo of Living Faith World Outreach, Lagos, Nigeria once said: *"An effective pulpit must become the gate of heaven where sinking souls are pulled out of the pits of life."*

The context of a minister maintaining balance is found in his/her ability and professionalism preaching, teaching and admonishing people *"to edification, and exhortation and comfort."* [20]

Escape for thy Life

These are *not* the times to sympathize with a *fluke* minister, nor get emotionally glued to that ministry because of your financial investments therein. Your soul is of an unquantifiable value before God. God's warning to Lot in Genesis 19:17 could well apply here. He was admonished:

> *"Escape for thy life; look not behind thee, neither stay thou in all the plain; escape to the mountain, lest thou be consumed."*

False prophets couldn't work with God's Holy Spirit – or rather, the latter wouldn't work with the former! So they had always resorted to deploying familiar, enchantment and divination spirits! They had succeeded in ensnaring countless gullible, unwary thousands. This seems to be our generation's sin: the insatiable desire to experience the world of spiritism – and the flocking after Satan's false prophets.

> *"For such are false apostles, deceitful workers, transforming themselves into the apostles of Christ.*
>
> *And no marvel: for Satan himself is transformed into an angel of light."*

2 CORINTHIANS 11:13–14

Receive the strength in the name of Christ Jesus to break free from controlling and manipulative spirits – and the bondages that have ensnared your potentials for so long!

God's Two Main Agents of Deliverance: The Angel(s) Dispatched

Idolatry was not just the only plague in the land. Another of Gideon's generation's problems was fear that swallowed up the word of faith God's prophet had brought them:

"And it came to pass, when the children of Israel cried unto the LORD because of the Midianites,

That the LORD sent a prophet unto the children of Israel …

And I said unto you, I am the LORD your God; fear not the gods of the Amorites, in whose land ye dwell: but you have not obeyed my voice."

JUDGES 6:8-10

It's amazing how we can become paralyzed by fear!

Fear of the inevitable plundering and destruction in the hands of the seasonal, merciless Midianitish raiders had shut the ears of the children of Israel to the message of faith. The Bible quantified the enemy number in Judges 6:5:

"For they came up with their cattle and their tents, and they came as grasshoppers for multitude; for both they and their camels were without number: and they entered into the land to destroy it."

The men of sight had only seen hordes of invaders – and not the potential deliverance God's word brings.

Isn't that like you when you are surrounded by negative circumstances?

The mail man delivers his rounds – but you're too scared to open the letter box! The phone rings, and it's the voice of the creditor at the other end asking for an unfailing settlement, by a set date. Maybe the bailiff has knocked your door – with a promise to return with a pick-axe! Probably, your home is about to be re-possessed or fore-closed. Your circumstance could be that you have recently received a bad health-report from the doctor!

You know, at times like this, when all you can see and hear are bad reports printed in white and black or red - or the trotting sounds of the approaching hooves of *hordes of enemies'* horses, the normal tendency is for *a* heart to sink. Our faith level automatically drops!

One quick thing Father God will do is activate the *supernatural* to invade our *natural*. He would auto-boost the ministry of His holy angels to correct our *eye-and-ear-defects* in order to re-capture our attention. He would authorize a miracle to re-establishing the incontestable fact that He, God, is *still* absolutely in control.

In Judges 6:11 we read: *"And there came an angel of the LORD, and sat under an oak which was in Ophrah ..."*

Moses, too, like you had lost focus. But God corrected his *eye-and-ear defects.* He refocused him through the ministry of the angel in the burning bush in Horeb, the mountain of God. Forty years earlier, Moses had caught the impression that God would use him as the emancipator of the Israelite bondage in Egypt. But he jumped before his time; and more, in his ability. He had suddenly and un-intentionally become Egypt's Number One Wanted Murder-convict. He had to run. And to Midian. Here, he was safe away from the long hands of the Egyptian extradition possibility. From palatial education and civilization, he prepared to adjust to *shepherdic* rurali-zation backside of the desert. What a way God pre-serves and equips His chosen vessels!

> *"Now Moses kept the flock of Jethro his father in law, the priest of Midian: and he led the flock to the backside of the desert, and came to the mountain of God, even to Horeb."*

Exodus 3:1

How would you feel, if by sovereign circumstances God allows a delay in the fulfillment of your original ambitions and visions of youth?

Many of the *jelly* christians of today would spend the rest of their lives depressed. But the Spirit of God and your conscience bear you witness that the clay ought not to protest the Potter's designs!

You couldn't have sunk as low as Moses had!

Moses, originally groomed to become the next Phar-aoh was now hiding. He'd have been jobless, but for the face-saving offer of his father-in-law to him to tend his sheep. Not only did he tend Jethro's sheep, he was sheltered by Jethro! (I wonder what kind of a son-in-law Moses had suddenly become.) He'd had his entire personality *arrested*; his head, very low.

Here, indeed, was the very crucible that would shapen him to compete for *God's Award of the Meekest Man on the Earth* contest. He would win that award in the next forty years or so!

It so happened, one day, in God's *fullness of time* unknown to him while he continued his daily rut having resigned his vision to fate, God dazzled and re-corrected Moses' lenses. He sent deliverance his way. God sent *His* angel:

> *"And the angel of the LORD appeared unto him in a flame of fire out of the midst of a bush: and he looked, and, behold, the bush burned with fire, and the bush was not consumed.*
>
> *And Moses said, I will now turn aside, and see this great sight, why the bush is not burnt."*

> EXODUS 3:2–3

That was Moses' day. May you also possess the patience much needed for the moment *your day* will arrive!

Gideon, much like Moses had abandoned himself into the hands of God, while he had faithfully carried on with the task for the moment. He had lived a day at a time. This is a great lesson for those who have adopted the get-all-or-loose-all mental approach to life. We are not to resign to life in moments of bereavement, a loss, an adversity or a delayed fulfillment of an aspiration. Rather we are to re-assign and reorder our lives and work our possible best within the permissible framework presented us while we earnestly hope and trust God to open a better door than there currently is availed unto us!

Gideon *had* to hide, but he *had* threshed wheat. More-often than not therefore, a place of profitable *busy-ness* even while in waiting has always been the place of encountering the divine.

> *"And there came an angel of the LORD, and sat under an oak which was in Ophrah, that pertained unto Joash the Abiezrite: and his son Gideon threshed wheat by the winepress, to hide it from the Midianites."*

This pivotal verse of scripture above is impregnated with spiritual truths. From it we derive:

- There came an angel of the LORD;
- Who sat under an Oak tree;
- Located at Ophrah, (an exact location in the city);
- Bearing the particular 'ID' of the beneficiary.

Seeking for an Angel versus the Appearance of an Angel

God created Mankind as wholly, spirit-beings with a desire and hunger to worship Him. He created us higher than angels in hierarchy; it is an abhorrence to seek or worship the lower beings!

All through the scriptures, God's angels had always being sent by God consequent upon His children's cry unto Him for divine assistance. Heaven will deploy

57

Her holy angels to execute God's redemptive purposes on the face of the Earth! Whenever *any* provokes the heart of God in worship – either positively or negatively, God's angels automatically show up. King Solomon had done just that at the dedication of the Jerusalem temple. [21] In the book of Acts, we read of the story of the wicked King Herod who had assumed the place of God. Immediately, God's angel struck him in judgment; he was eaten up by worms! [22]

If you become desperate in your search of spirits, you will be led to witness falsehood. Such *hocus-pocus*, spooky appearances or apparitions – which are all demonic, will be your *gain* and pain!

These days witness an increase in people's inquisitive, insatiable desire to peep into the spirit world via the séances, Ouija board, crystal ball, yoga, extra sensory travel, *(EST's)* and the mediums. More accessible in trado-African sense are the alfas, imams, native witch doctors – and infact, *spiritist* churches where angels' names are deployed in prayer, as a prerequisite to access the Heavenly Father. The Word of God however clearly declares that *"there is none other name given among men, whereby we must be saved."* [23] In Philippians 2:9–10, we are hinted of the only potent legal name in the entire Universe by which we must call on God: it is the name of Jesus!

> *"Wherefore God hath highly exalted him and given him a name which is above every name:*

*That at the name of Jesus every knee should bow, of
things in heaven, and things in earth, and things
under the earth."*

Gaining entrance (or attempting to enter) into the
spirit realm through another name, means or person
other than JESUS CHRIST, the Son of the living God
is demonic!

If you are saved however, you may send *your* angel on
an assignment by the word of the Lord. The scripture
teaches that the angels of God are ministering spirits
sent forth to minister to them who shall be heirs of
salvation. [24] God's angels are our *spiritual aids.*

Angels possess accurate information about us that
we may *not* even be aware of personally. And unlike
homo sapiens, Heaven's angels will not deploy their
superior knowledge to *hurt* us but rather soothe our
hurts. Dr. Billy Graham had aptly titled one of his
classics referring to angels as *God's Secret Agents.* And
being God's secret agents, angels know our most
secret insecurities, hurts and frustrations.

In my personal life, home and ministry, I have been a
beneficiary of angelic ministration many times. I
envision angels as *benders, fenders and menders.* A
concise angelic intervention I witnessed October
1999. We'd passed the night at a friend minister's
home. I'd thought of easing the pressing urge to visit
the toilet for a *'short call'*; so I'd placed my daughter
Gabby – barely thirteen months – on a six-foot high
bunk, farthest away from the ladder. I had forgotten

how inquisitive the little lady could be. From that disadvantaged position, Gabby had taken a dive. All I had heard, four or five quick steps away from the room, were the delightful, squeaky sounds produced by a child being tickled.

Instinctively, my urge for the toilet suddenly disappeared. I'd spun around and dashed for the high bunk-bed. It had all happened within two to three seconds, *earth time*. What I'd witnessed astounded me: there on the floor sat a cheerful baby giggling at me. No bruise. No hurts. No cries, only full of smiles. [25]

I couldn't have been more grateful for the watchful eyes of our Heavenly Father – and the services of our *secret agents*.

Where Gideon's Angel Sat

Gideon's angel had sat under an oak tree in Ophrah on a land portion owned by Joash, Gideon's father. There is a symbolic truth here which the Lord called my attention unto about the positioning of God's angel – that is, under an oak tree in the center of the city.

Now, oak trees take hundreds of years or more to grow and mature. But once matured, they are a very strong tree. An oak therefore signifies strength, endurance or formidableness.

Earlier, we have seen that it was the generational habit of the Israelites in Gideon's days to hide away from their enemies. Gideon himself was in hiding. It would certainly be true to notice that such places where God usually dispatches His angels are places of weakness, helplessness, frustration, barrenness, oppression or limitation.

Heaven is not going to watch you go through those low ebbs of life – and throw you a wave of the hand, dismissing and laughing at you. Rather, God will dispatch His secret service agents – the angels – to your rescue. Being armed with this truth places you a step ahead of any of the schemes and ploys of the wicked one!

Are you cast down, helpless, lonely, fearful, frustrated or hopeless?

Know this: God is nearest. His angels are most present. But your reaction to Him in the face of adversity must be that of reaching out to Him in prayers with an expectation. Not *with* complaints. Not with murmuring nor grumbling – nor indeed, with a wrong attitude!

'Stinker' Attitudes Prevent the Miraculous from Occurring

Some attitudes we – christians – exhibit in trial times will qualify for a *stinker!* For instance, we are confronted by a giant, and instead of running to our Father; we turn our backs *on* Him. We tackle issues of life in our wisdom. Soon, things hardly work out – and we are quick to apportion Him blame. Some of us are actually audacious enough to tell Father God how disgusted we are with Him if He delays to answer our prayers in time – and on *our* terms. We question His authority and ability.

Some neglect prayer and the study of God's word – privately and publicly, in fellowship. They moan, complain and get bitter about the church, the pastors and the brethren. So, they abstain from attending services, lock themselves indoors – and possibly contemplate suicide.

Your attitude stinks!

Because *your* attitude stinks, God could *not* avail His angels the authorization codes to your release and deliverance. The inviting fragrances God loves to inhale are contained in the golden vials of the saints' importunate prayers and sacrificial offerings! [26]

Consider these Saints' *fragrances*

Consider Queen Esther's confidence *in* God when she approached King Ahasuerus, uncalled. Her bravery called for Heaven's intervention to save a whole generation of Jews! But she first took her very own life in her mouth. [27]

Consider Shadrach, Meshach and Abednego; the three Hebrew children were delivered from Nebuchadnezzar's fiery furnace, but their salvation wouldn't be possible first, without their determination to proceed into the flames! Only once they had been hurled in did they discover that *here*, indeed, was Heaven's appointed place to dazzle Babylon with one of the recorded, historical *physical* appearances of the very Son of God! [28]

Jesus says, *"whosoever will save his life will loose it; but whosoever shall lose his life for my sake and the gospel's, the same shall save it."* [29]

Consider Daniel. He had dared to confront the unjust order of the Babylonian House of Parliament forbidding anyone praying to the God of Heaven! He would suffer the consequences of such *a* confrontation of the law: into the hungry lions' den, he would go. But the holy God of Heaven intervened; He sent His angel to the den. The angel had locked the mouths of the lions in the den. They couldn't do God's servant any harm. [30] What a mighty God we serve!

*Wouldn't you love to take a stance for **this** God, today?*

Consider imprisoned Peter. Peter's imprisonment chains fell off and the iron gates of the prison opened of their own accord, at the sight of God's angel. But Herod had just executed James – and had thought Peter was next. [31]

Friend, Father God is honored when He sees us *size up* against the devil; yet thump our chests, boasting, that we have a Father Who is always present. A Father Who will never leave nor forsake us – and more, a Father, able to deliver us. Suddenly, spells of formidable opposition, generational curses, unfathomed sicknesses, afflictions and bondages are broken at His intervention; our weakest points therefore, transformed into junctions of strength.

Chapter 4

Junctions of Transformation

"A man's greatest strength develops at the point where he overcomes his greatest weakness."

- ELMER G. LETTERMAN

Thus far, we have seen the need for us to *dig around* our decayed *roots*. We have also established the importance of our importunate prayers – coupled with the right attitude; the preserving influence of *the* God-sent prophet in our lives, and the inevitable ministry of God's *secret agents* to us, the angels. Still awaiting our assault, though, are the junctions of transformation we must resolutely cross.

What is a Junction of Transformation?

A junction of transformation is often a place of great

strife – and subsequently, the place of our conse-
quential overcoming of our greatest weakness. We
each have *that* battle to do – and *that* junction to cross
– if *our* potentials must be fully unfurled!

Jacob's destiny was at stake. His fraudulent character
had ever been his limiting factor. However, this
inherent-from-birth trait would be changed only in a
momentous decisive all-night-long battle with the
Almighty God.

Jacob realized his potential. But he equally figured
out that for him to attain the best he was created to
be, he probably *had* a battle to fight. There at Peniel,
God announced to him, including those – who have
come to terms with the undeniable fact that *they* have
a battle at hand – the outcome of the contest:

> *"And he said, Thy name shall be called no more*
> *Jacob, but Israel: for as a prince hast thou power*
> *with God and with men, and hast prevailed."*

GENESIS 32:28

Notice with me, two great keys God announced
Jacob – newly named Israel – now possesses:

"for as a prince hast thou power with God and with men."

First, he possessed the key of influence.

We will *not* possess power, influence or authority
with men except we attain power, influence and
authority first, *with* God. This power, we achieve, in
prevailing prayers.

Second, Jacob earned a scar!

Guard the loins of your mind. Anyone emerging victorious from this destiny-shaping battleground of transformation shall necessarily emerge, wearing a scar! There will necessarily be a *sign* to show for your encounter with the Divine! This scar, most often times, is actually not easily visible to the naked eyes!

You see, God allows His anointed to wear scars so as to help them keep in mind the moment they traversed *that* junction of transformation. Another reason God allows saints to be branded is to keep them humble. Israel attained power and prevailed with God but not without a halt to his walk! [1] Apostle Paul too emerged victorious in his many encounters with the Lord; albeit, with many a scar. [2]

Gideon's Quest for Transformation

We are informed of Gideon's quest for transformation in Judges 6:12–15:

> *"And the angel of the LORD appeared unto him, and said unto him, The LORD is with thee, thou mighty man of valour.*
>
> *And Gideon said unto him, Oh my Lord, if the LORD be with us, why then is all this befallen us? and where be all his miracles which our fathers told us of, saying, Did not the LORD bring us up from Egypt? but now the LORD hath forsaken us, and delivered us into the hands of the Midianites.*

And the LORD looked upon him, and said, Go in this thy might, and thou shalt save Israel from the hand of the Midianites: have not I sent thee?

And he said unto him, Oh my Lord, wherewith shall I save Israel? behold, my family is poor in Manasseh, and I am the least in my father's house.

And the LORD said unto him, Surely I will be with thee, and thou shalt smite the Midianites as one man."

Here, we notice few but pronounced junctions of transformation awaiting Gideon's assailing vis-à-vis *insecurity, poverty* and *spiritual inaptitude!*

Shall we examine them, each?

1. Gideon's Insecurity

In Judges 6, four distinct times did God commend Gideon and charge him. Summarily for Gideon though, ten times did he renounce God's commendations. This was Gideon's perception of himself: two-and-a-half times lower than God's perception of him. Mathematically speaking, that would be a negative *2.5 scale of enlargement.*

More, *our* Gideon would offer excuses to the Almighty – and even conduct *faith-experiments* when doubts and fears assailed him!

Surely, these signs only point to one sure fact: Gideon was a deeply, insecure man.

Earlier, in the Israelites' history – and bid to enter Canaan – Moses had sent twelve spies ahead, (a spy per tribe), to espy the land God had promised to give to Abraham. These spies were to submit their findings within forty days. Ten spies had brought damning, evil reports, against the report of Caleb and Joshua. In Numbers 13:32–33 we read:

> *"And they brought up an evil report of the land which they had searched unto the children of Israel, saying, The land, through which we have gone to search it, is a land that eateth up the inhabitants thereof; and all the people that we saw in it are men of a great stature.*
>
> *And there we saw the giants, the sons of Anak, which come of the giants: and we were in our own sight as grasshoppers, and so we were in their sight."*

Did you notice their perception issues?

For forty days, they envisioned themselves as grasshoppers. That sealed their fate. God was only faithful enough to bid their destinies what imagination they themselves had conceived.

Do you now see how important it is for us to necessarily possess **the right perception** *of ourselves?*

What is *the* right perception of me?

How do I *find* it?

The right perception of a person cannot be set by the societal norms and values. Neither can it be set by the images and expectations espoused through the media or exotic magazines on the news-stands/shelves. *The right perception of you is that perception God sees and declares about you! You search and find it in the Word of God! Until you locate God's perception of you, you remain blind, purposeless and aimless.*

God's verdict on the *blind* congregation in the wilderness?

> *"Say unto them, As truly as I live, saith the LORD, as ye have spoken in mine ears, so will I do to you:*
>
> *Your carcases shall fall in this wilderness: and all that were numbered of you, according to your whole number, from twenty years old and upwards, which have murmured against me."*

NUMBERS 14:28–29

Hundreds of thousands of them were wasted in the wilderness. Here is another lesson for us: we must jealously guard what thoughts ruminate within our minds – including the words of our soliloquy or quiet moments. God is listening. His tapes are running!

> *"... if thou hast thought evil, lay thine hand upon thy mouth"*

PROVERBS 30:32

> *"... as he thinketh in his heart, so is he ..."*

PROVERBS 23:7

The teenaged shepherd, David, I thought ought rather to have perceived of himself as *a grasshopper* in comparison with the great Goliath. Neither David's stature nor Goliath's were of equal rankings; their shoulders and voice pitches were never in near comparison!

Instead of gaining an actual perception of the scenario, David chose to gain an Heavenly perception! It is as simple as that.

You also have the choice to make: swap the negative, actual images of your real life challenges with Heaven's pre-declared outcomes. For instance, *you* would swap the doctor's report with your Heavenly Father's declaration of health. *You* would decree the salvation of *your* children that have suddenly turned wayward, while they are yet in rebellion against God! Whatever the situation that stares you in the face, you have the power to make a deliberate choice to swap earthly images with Heaven's pre-determined, pre-declared counsel of victory!

David had a solid understanding of this principle. He made the right choice. He conceived of the battle outcome in his mind, and declared the victory with his tongue, even before the battle commenced. These were his brave words to the Philistine 'buffy-slayer':

> *"This day will the LORD deliver thee into mine hand; and I will smite thee and take thine head from thee; and I will give the carcases of the host of the Philistines this day unto the fowls of the air,*

> *and to the wild beasts of the earth; that all the earth may know that there is a God in Israel."*

1 SAMUEL 17:46

How prophetic those words were!

God honored *little* David's right perception both of himself – and his God, just as He would honor yours!

Ponder with me. *What kind of self-perception do you portray to the heavenly realms when you resort to begging for money either in private or public, for personal or ministerial purposes?* Yet, worse still, some christian people borrow with the intention never to repay that which they have borrowed!

What perceptions have you, when you continue to amass credit card debts – and set yourself up for financial strangulation?

One watchword will re-position you towards Heaven's favor. That word is *control*.

Dare to control your spending. Curb your excesses. Draw up a budget. Control what you buy without cash. Devise means to ensure you live within your means. Ask for debt counseling.

Never drive under the influence of alcohol; nor slide behind the steering wheel without purchasing an insurance cover. (These reckless acts could prove fatal for you, your family – and indeed, others!)

Swap the image of your self-perception to that of

God's perception of you. You are *the* child of the King! You're a prince/princess of the Kingdom of Heaven. Why live beggarly and 'wantonly'? Why would you want to knot a noose round your neck apart from a fine dressing tie? [3]

Conditions Giving Rise to Insecurities

A few conditions could give birth to insecurity in any person. Foremost is the person's *defective* background, if not corrected.

Gideon's insecurity, as we have seen, was fathered by a defective background of hiding caused by years of historical cycles of sin, shame and defeat.

Your insecure feelings could have resulted from deep guilt feelings of earlier sins. Some children's emotions have been battered and scarred since childhood. They have been molested by parents or relatives – or the very trusted people, meant to have shielded them from harm! Such kids grow into dysfunctional adults – who also become violators. Except they encounter the Healer Christ, they will hurt through their lifetime!

Some others have not been openly battered, but have been secretly betrayed. This betrayal could have arisen as a result of an absent father or mother; parents too busy at work had traded quality time – meant for their children in those crucial, early formative years – for money. The children grow up feeling unloved and rejected – despite all the toys and gifts showered on them! Such kids develop into a hollow shell of an emotional personality; they grow up resentful, bitter and angry!

Furthermore, insecure feelings may result from the frustrations emanating from seemingly fruitless years of enduring a rut of a life-style, job – or even ministry. Years of abuse in a bad marriage/relationship may also leave the abused with deep wounds!

What of the untold frustration in an un-channeled bachelorhood, spinsterhood, widowhood, widower-hood or divorce? This frustration may set in motion, fear. Fear may prolong singleness which ends in loneliness. The mystery surrounding loneliness is that *it* knows no bounds. Anyone could become lonely. *Westerners* – by any means are the loneliest people on the face of the earth. (Mother Teresa called loneliness, "the leprosy of the West"). A wealthy married person may be lonely. You may even be lonely in the midst of a large family!

As you read this, a child may be running away from home: this is in their childish mind, a bid to escape the built-up pressures, shame, frustrations and insecurities co-habiting that home with the legal residents. A spouse may be tempted to walk away from the marriage they had labored for all their life!

In the face of these nerve-breaking piles of ever-changing pressures upon a soul, what would God demand of such beleaguered soul?

God's expectation of such a soul is found in Hebrew 6:11–12:

> *"And we desire that every one of you do shew the same diligence to the full assurance of hope unto the end:*
>
> *That ye be not slothful, but followers of them who through faith and patience inherit the promises."*

We are admonished to *not* become overwhelmed, but be followers. We are told to become meticulous students of success stories: people who through faith and patience inherited God's promises!

For example, the priest Zecharias, barren and past age, was a man fully exercised in temperance and determined faithfulness. He endured and received the promise of a baby named John the Baptist, who became the fore-runner of the Messiah of the world! Joseph was another classical example of godly resilience. He endured thirteen years of shame in prison for a false fornication charge leveled against him. In the end, he emerged victorious. From prison, he moved into the palace.

God will not lower His *Quality Control Tests* because of *you.* Patience, perseverance, and a healthy outlook brought about by hope in God will surely enhance your resoluteness assaulting life's many a junction of transformation.

The Subtle Danger of Insecurity

Insecurity is ruthless. It always deals deathly blows to its victims.

Insecurity in the strong makes him bow to the weak. It makes a mother 'cover up' her daughter's misdeeds that she may not loose the daughter's favor. Insecurity makes the father forcefully marry his daughter to the undeserving.

Insecure personality feelings make a youth abuse the expensive perfume in a bid to attract the opposite sex. Insecurity has suffocated and repressed many a great destiny that would have mattered for God. It has stifled what would hitherto have been great potentials for the Kingdom.

Insecurity drove *"a mighty man of valour"* like Gideon to retreat into hiding. It had drowned the mightiness in him.

Insecurity made King Saul rebel against God's commands to utterly destroy the Amalekites for having denied Israel a thorough fare across their land *en route* Canaan. That single act of Saul's disobedience marred thirty-eight years of good reign. The king had embarked on a descent via a tumultuous, two year, quick, spiral journey that eventually saw him below the bottom.

Furthermore, insecurity – in whatever form – could nudge its victims to do the most absurd things. For instance, a teenage girl had committed suicide because a boyfriend had jilted her.

The cause?

A careless *off-the-wall* comment he'd made to her

girlfriend bordering on issues regarding his girl-friend shedding 'excess weight.'

In a dramatic twist, another girl had been driven to become anorexic because of inner yearnings to attain the implausible size zero!

A madam had been trapped by a huge indebtedness in her bid to acquire the latest wears, more exclusive than her neighbor's.

And only at the start of the *Y2K*, a group in a country in Europe began to campaign for their right to appear nude in public places like the parks, supermarkets, streets – and even, offices!

In the ministry, this wicked venom of insecurity rouses us up and makes us want to outclass each other – if not probably tarnish another's image with a negative, punitive comment. Some pastors had even ordered militia-like men from theirs to embarrass – in threatening behaviors and conduct – the leaders from the other church. Some of you have been incensed to tear down the opposing church's valid posters for no just cause!

How far can we advance Heaven's interests in these 'maddened', confused states of being?

Gideon's insecurity had turned him into an extremely unstable, disbelieving character. He could not believe God's word despite repeated assurances. He could not even believe in himself, let alone another. Now, such people at this verge of lost faith in

God, others and themselves could endear quick disaster to any, nearby them.

A young man from an educated pedigree in one of our great Universities many years ago was privileged to hold a U.S citizenship by birth. He had been in and out of America on a good number of occasions. But the other day he traveled out, there was only one *souvenir* he brought with him home: a .38 Colt revolver with a muffler. How he managed to sneak it out of one country and into another, no one knows!

"What for, with all those opportunities before him?" you may ask.

Well, he shot himself in the head with that gun. He ended his life partly because of his *insecurity issues.* Other partly, because of his selfishness. His suicide he thought, would be a source of torment to his kindred who made him feel so insecure.

For Gideon, towards the end of his life, it was obvious that his insecurity problem not once earlier dealt with *did* eventually ensnare him. Immediately, after the Midianites' defeat by the Israeli army he had led, Gideon had become a war hero. That was many years ago. Today, he'd become old – perhaps lonely and forsaken; yet, he relished the memories of power he'd wielded decades earlier. So the masses asked him if he would like to run for a second term in office at *"a good old age."* [4]

The masses were careful and sensitive to coax out of him, his innermost yearning to be hero-worshipped.

When he declined outright, their consensus referendum vote for his re-governance of Israel, that move was clearly understandable. Age was not on his side. The people had only looked for an avenue to arouse his ego. In a carefully contrived plot however, they eventually were able to hatch his secret desire: Gideon began to clamor for a monument in recognition of his past achievement. The children of Israel pretended to succumb to his whimpering call for a *"Golden Monumental Memory of General Gideon's Achievement in Israel."* This turned out to be Gideon's costliest mistake; second only to the Gibeonites' deception he'd earlier fallen prey to.

> *"And Gideon made an ephod thereof, and put it in his city, even in Ophrah: and all Israel went thither a whoring after it: which thing became a snare unto Gideon and to his house."*

JUDGES 6:27

Ophrah, the place of Gideon's rising had also become the place of his falling just because of his "hero-worship-me" insecurity issues that he'd pretended never existed deep within him!

Steve Farrar in his book *Finishing Strong* did make reference to Dr. Robert Clinton's study of leaders. Dr. Clinton had categorized leaders into these groups: *cut off early, finished poorly, finished "so-so"* and *finished well.*

You won't be surprised to note that Gideon had been categorized among the "finished poorly" group, alongside Eli, Saul and Solomon.

Is there any Gideon buried deep within the deep recesses of your heart?

Are there any long existent issues deeply buried within you which you are denying were ever underlaid?

Search your very heart; let *go* of them today – and rather, let godliness be sown instead!

2. Gideon's Poverty

In Judges 6:14–15 we read:

> *"And the LORD looked upon him, and said, Go in this thy might, and thou shalt save Israel from the hand and of the Midianites: have not I sent thee?*
>
> *And he said unto him Oh my Lord, wherewith shall I save Israel? behold, my family is poor in Manasseh, and I am the least in my father's house."*

Whenever God has chosen any, His yardstick has more than often been to choose from the undeserving, the broken, the lowly – and sometimes, the unqualified! The reason He does this is to ensure that no other being takes the credit or glory due to Him alone. If you happen to originate from the high caste, and God's eyes are set on you for His use, be sure He will pass you through his filters! We read in 1 Corinthians 1:26–29:

"For ye see your calling, brethren, how that not many wise men after the flesh, not many mighty, not many noble, are called:

But God hath chosen the foolish things of the world to confound the wise; and God hath chosen the weak things of the world to confound the things which are mighty;

And base things of the world, and things which are despised, hath God chosen, yea, and things which are not, to bring to nought things that are:

That no flesh should glory in his presence."

Gideon was overwhelmed by God's awesome presence and commission. But an agitation at the back of his mind was the issue of his abject poverty! He retorted at the angel: *"Wherewith shall I save Israel?"*

In Gideon we find poverty of **means**, **men** and **mastery**.

Could this be your experience today?

Poverty of *means* – in particular – is the crucial, make-or-break junction of transformation for most new entrepreneurs, pastors or missionaries on foreign fields. It is saddening, however, that not a few have made a shipwreck of their calling, trying to negotiate this notorious split-junction.

They've either bastardized Heaven's avowed prosperity message because of their greed; or they've utterly rejected the divine provision Heaven avails probably because of their pride or ignorance of such availability.

Still, a few dare compromise altogether the true Gospel, for money! [5]

Throughout the history of the spread of the Gospel despite blatant attacks the message has suffered, we are assured of a certainty: God gloriously executes the projects He has assigned! [6]

The Importance of Money

God's word is unbiased in its teachings, verifying the importance of money in achieving God's purposes on earth! For instance, we read through the wisest man ever lived that *"money answereth all things."* [7]

Let us be practical. Now; *'Are mere clouds without rain of any vital significance to a farmer in an arid land?'* The answer is an emphatic *'No!'*

To further buttress the point of the necessity of cash inflow in ultimately realizing destinies, I will refer to the poignant short story told by King Solomon. In this story, there was a poor wise man who possessed the wisdom to deliver a city from under the siege of a strong, great king. Nevertheless, his *real* potential remained stifled – and his name unremembered because of lack of finance/cash. Read it with me:

> *"There was a little city, and few men within it; and there came a great king against it, and besieged it, and built great bulwarks against it:*

Now there was found in it a poor wise man, and he by his wisdom delivered the city; yet no man remembered that same poor man.

Then said I, Wisdom is better than strength: nevertheless the poor man's wisdom is despised, and his words are not heard."

ECCLESIASTES 9:14-16

You see, a poor man is always put to shame – and will be more than often disappointed in the end.

Poverty always contains a man well behind schedule. Poverty robs a person of their dignity! There is absolutely nothing dignifying about poverty; poverty is certainly ungodly! It is a curse to conceive master plans – yet die with such concepts and with witty abilities just for lack of expression.

The Bible says that the poor, wise man's words were *not* heard because he lacked the means to make them heard! In other words, he led an unfulfilled, un-rewarded life and destiny!

The availability to a person or ministry of money, materials and manpower – in their rightful places – are like a workman's tools in the hands of the Almighty God. Yet still, His overall authority must be sought, even, on our engagement and deployment of these *tools*. God must continually be afforded the ultimate supremacy and glory. We possess these *tools* because *He* gave them to us; and not the *tools* possessing us because we are given to them!

> *"Except the Lord build the house, they labour in vain that build it: except the LORD keep the city, the watchman waketh but in vain."*

PSALMS 127:1

One of my many concerns, however, is that even though God may be rightly placed in the plans of our hearts; often times, we just want to *arrive* big over-night! Truthfully, I am more persuaded that *"this wisdom descendeth not from above, but is earthly, sensual, devilish."* [8]

Let me illustrate what I mean with these graphic details of Gabby, while she was growing up:

For the first 6 months, she was very observant - and a keen watcher.

Next half year, she was an active participant at almost all activities of children her age.

Ages 12–18 months she began to mumble a few words. She also started learning to perfect her balance – followed by subsequent walking. (She did not crawl though; she just rose up on her feet someday at 14 months, ran round a small circle a couple of times before falling on her bottom. She was soon up again, beaming wide smiles, proud of her very own achievements!)

Ages 18–24 months she learned faster, repeating after us anything she picked in surrounding conversations and *hear-says*. (Soon she also began to walk faster.

Sometimes, she would take off as an airplane on the runway; fall, cry and yell – only to re-commence running again!)

36 months after birth, she was an expert communicator and runner. She would even gesticulate with her hands, shoulders, eyes, and head – sometimes, probably employing matured *body languages* inspite of the fact that no one ever sat her down through a lecture on how to express oneself through viable *body languages!*

I am persuaded to believe that this is a vivid illustration of a God ordained growth process – that could slightly vary from child to child. And yet, though a female, she cannot be expected to carry a baby until she is matured, established and wedded – and that in the next two decades! But would you pause to note that this single life started all out just a *seed* of two gametes!

How amazing God *does* multiply, in His time!

In Acts 5, we learned that the high powered Sanhedrin Council's machinery was soon going to attempt shredding the Jerusalem Church. Seeing their imminent threat; God, from among their inner circle raised up an eminent member named Gamaliel. Unknown to the rest, he was a secret admirer of the Master, Jesus Christ. The Heavens filled his mouth with sage counsel. This story is told in Acts 5:34–39. Here are some excerpts of that memorable speech made by Doctor Gamaliel that helped clog the rumbling engine of the enemy's *shredder machine* to a standstill:

> *"Ye men of Israel, take heed to yourselves what ye intend to do as touching these men.*
>
> *And now I say unto you, Refrain from these men, and let them alone: for if this counsel or this work be of men, it will come to nought:*
>
> *But if it be of God, ye cannot overthrow it; lest haply ye be found even to fight against God."*

VERSES 35; 38–39

No matter the magnitude of hell's attack against a godly seed, that seed will germinate, grow and blossom! This is because the tiniest of Heaven's seeds bears Haven's overcoming genetic codes. God's Word says that whatsoever is born of God overcomes whatever restraints the *cosmos*, the devil and his cohorts have to throw at it! [9]

Are you born of God? Do you carry heaven's genetic codes within you?

God enabled me hurdle forever another crucial transformation junction early December 2000. He had been scaling me past preparatory heights since a few years now, as far as I can remember. On Monday November 6, 2000 my seventy-year old father slipped away into eternity. Being the elder of the two children immediately accessible of the three surviving kids, the onus of responsibility passed onto me, without pre-warning. After extensive consultations with families and church ministers, burial date was fixed for fixed for thirty-two days later, December 8th.

A fortnight to this date, no money had flowed in. Shame looked inevitable. I only did what God's wisdom directed me to do. So, I called my younger sister, and asked us to pray to the Heavenly Father!

We knelt at my study table and its chair – which had now shrunk and grown moldy, due to dis-use over the years since leaving home. There, by these pieces of furniture, we raised an altar to the Lord!

Same afternoon, shortly, a telephone call came through. A tax-free sum of $2000USD was in the bank. Five days later, our family Church – where dad had served as an elder for over forty years – sent us a check for 30 000 local currency. Soon, individuals' gifts also trickled in, by their thousands. By the burial date, all was ready!

The funeral ceremony was excellent, decent and peaceful. God had proved His providence unto us. A total estimated sum of N350 000 had passed through our hands in just a matter of two weeks. *Nay-sayers'* mouths were completely shut. (A distant cousin who was poised to cause trouble, we later gathered, was stuck on the highway as his convoy of exotic cars suddenly developed engine faults. None of the inhabitants of a convoy of four cars *did* attend the party. They arrived a day after *all* ceremonies had been concluded - all in smelly clothes, smothered in thick black engine oil!)

I took a look at them – and smiled. It was a victorious smile!

We did not beg, crawl nor were indebted.

What can't our God do?

After God took me past this testimony of a six figure expense just shared, I knew deep within me that I had just forever navigated another crucial junction of transformation. I knew that I could never be poor, ever again!

If God did it for me, He will do it for you too. He will embarrass all your financial embarrassments in Jesus' mighty name.

Now, not only did Gideon lack *means,* **he lacked** *effective manpower.*

We were informed that he had at most ten trained, reliable and dependable men. [10] Certainly, this number was pitiable and would be suicidal to marshal against the Midianites who *"came as grasshoppers for multitude."* [11]

Are you a Gideon business-person, a Gideon-minister, a lonely, despised, barren woman? Today I have a word from heaven for you: God will surprise and multiply you abundantly, *if* you will remain consistently faithful!

Gideon's God would soon raise for Himself an army. How He would do it however, he was not pre-informed.

In Ezekiel's time, God's Spirit took the prophet on a trip to a vast graveyard in a dry valley full of dry dead men's bones – and assured the prophet, He (God) was able to make the dry bones live and form a mighty army! [12] Thus, a versatile army was raised from mere dead bones.

In this story vividly portrayed in Ezekiel 37, the Holy Spirit quickened me to realize that for God to eventually raise an army from this dry valley of total impossibility, He would employ the prophet's prophetic abilities!

We read in Ezekiel 37:3–4:

> *"And he said unto me, Son of man, can these bones live? And I answered, O Lord GOD, thou knowest.*
>
> *Again he said unto me, Prophesy upon these bones, and say unto them, O ye dry bones, hear the word of the LORD."*

At first, the prophet was instructed to *"prophesy"* upon the dry bones, *"the word of the Lord."* [13] These dry bones represent the skeletal framework of a vision, envisioned!

Next, the obedient prophet was nudged: *"Prophesy unto the wind, prophesy, son of man and say to the wind … breathe upon these slain, that they may live."* [14] The wind is symbolic of all elements that bring life to existence.

Notice, at each crucial stage of *his* army formation, Prophet Ezekiel was instructed to prophesy again and again unto the formidable impediments. Not complain. Not run about helplessly. Not panic in fear. Not flip the mobile set and call his best friend and confidante. *What am I trying to home in upon?* I am amplifying the need for you to use your tongue as an instrument of change – in your near impossible circumstance – by speaking the words of God!

Some people in an attempt to get solutions to pressing difficulties had related word to dream killers about their ministry, business, marriage or children.

But *not* Ezekiel. He only did say what God had put in his mouth to re-order *things* that never were, into *be-ing*!

> *"So I prophesied as I was commanded …"*

EZEKIEL 37:7

And the result?

> *"And when I beheld, lo, the sinews and the flesh came up upon them, and the skin covered them above: but there was no breath in them."*

VERSE 8

To make the bones live, still, Ezekiel must *not* relent in the use of his God-ordained prophetic abilities:

> *"Then said he unto me, Prophesy unto the wind, prophesy, son of man, and say to the wind, thus saith the Lord GOD; Come from the four winds, O breath, and breathe upon these slain, that they may live.*

> *So I prophesied as he commanded me, and the breath came into them, and they lived, and stood up upon their feet, an exceeding great army."*

EZEKIEL 37:11–12

Notice, the prophet's *forth-telling* abilities were *the* tool in the hands of God for raising for Himself an army! In the same manner, your mouth was not only primarily given you by God as a conduit through which food could get into your system, neither was your tongue made just for savoring a delicious meal or tasting a fine wine! Both the mouth and the tongue are an instrument of creation to those who are well-trained in their deployment to gainful, redemptive purposes – or indeed, death-inducing uses! God's Word says *"death and life and in the power of the tongue, and they who indulge in the use of it shall eat the fruit of it (for death or life)."* [15]

God's Varying Styles of Accomplishing His Purposes

While the end result remains God will ultimately perform what He'd promised He would, His methods of achieving His goals, from time to time, may vary! His choice of raising Gideon an army slightly varied from raising Ezekiel's – just as much as I am persuaded to believe it will be varied to raising yours. The primary truth is that God will Himself raise *an army* for his servant; *an army*, meet for use as a workman's tools, to bring His Kingdom the ultimate glory.

To raise Ezekiel's army, God tested the prophet's *obedience to prophesy*. For Gideon, God ascertained his *obedience to release*; to let go of the tens of hundreds whom he had conscripted into the *force*. That alone, was a huge transformation junction for Gideon!

Could it be that the Lord has allowed the choice of a person, place or circumstance in your life at this time, yet, they are however assuming to ascend the place of glory-taking over you?

Attain wisdom from Gideon! Letting go of *replicas* may be your smartest move that will usher in the *real deal*!

In ministry, most times, we are deluded by the *crowd effect*. Yes, huge crowds are enviable and desirable but the servant of God must not fix his heart upon the crowds of people, but the God who brought the crowd. God may be in the mammoth crowd, but the crowd may not always be *in* Christ. Remember the effect of crowd-clamor upon Moses' destiny in the Church in the wilderness! They stifled his potentials until they eventually robbed him of his destiny. (Mixed multitude untamed should be expected to exhibit just a little Satanism.)

In Gideon's experience, God needed only 300 worthy men out of the 32 000 who had answered the call for conscription. We read in Judges 7:2:

> *"And the LORD, said unto Gideon, The people that are with thee are too many for me to give the*

> *Midianites into their hands, lest Israel vaunt themselves against me, saying, Mine own hand hath saved me."*

God never had need of glory takers. This has always been His jealousy-guide post. He has always warned: *"I will not give my glory unto another."* [16] Simple subtractive math in Gideon's force thereof revealed 31 700 men as gleeful, tongue-in-the-cheek, joy-rider, *glory-seekers!*

Can you imagine 31 700 joy-rider, proud, boastful glory-takers as your share-holders in your new company?

This bunch was just a good-for-nothing mixt multitude. And where the opinions of a mixt multitude hold sway, "men praising" – a subtle idolatrous practice – would not be found wanting.

I pray for you today, that you receive enough strength to re-focus your eyes away from the seeming sources of help and support for the unfailing Everlasting arms alone.

Recognizing "mixt" multitude

Mixed multitude (written as *mixt* in King James Version) cannot be too hard to recognize by keen spiritual eyes. Some *'mixt folk'* solely depend upon their well-meaning connections for deliverance, to the detriment of their keeping close connection with God. Others, some, even choose church affiliation based upon the availability of 'juicy' folks who become their business contacts. For many, the subtle reason they attend church and become noticeable in subgroups is to essentially be able to find eligible spouses!

What a horrendous task a true shepherd must perform.

Yet, do you know, some, articulately skilled in instrumental *know-how* or voice inflexions flaunt their virtuosity and talents before the *highest bidder* Church? *"There ain't gonna be no show, without the real show!"* What a mediocre looser mentality unfurled!

A lively crowd of congregants, successful professionals and 'one-touch' influential powerful persons are only like chariots of war. We *need* them. But it is only the God of Heaven who places warriors on chariots. Not us!

The Word says the people who trust in chariots and horses are brought down and fallen. But those who trust in Jehovah God are forever standing! [17]

Gideon's loss of a lousy and greedy glory-taker group of *mixt folk* wasn't indeed a loss; rather, it was a tremendous earning for the Lord of Hosts – and His obedient servant. You may have circumvented your test for too long. It's 'time up!' Time to *let go, let God!*

3. Gideon's Spiritual Inaptitude

Gideon was not adept in spiritual matters. Nevertheless, he was open, sincere and willing to learn. Most apprentices these days are not so keen on learning. Some *under-shepherds* in young ministries are lesser than sincere.

It was Gideon's sincerity however, and openness to admit his fears that made him "double check" God's calling on his life. He therefore put out a fleece – and God honored him:

> *"And Gideon said unto God, If thou wilt save Israel by mine hand, as thou hast said.*
>
> *Behold, I will put a fleece of wool in the floor; and if the dew be on the fleece only, and it be dry upon all the earth beside, then shall I know that thou wilt save Israel by mine hand, as thou hast said.*
>
> *And it was so: for he rose up early on the morrow, and thrust the fleece together, and wringed the dew out of the fleece, a bowl full of water.*
>
> *And Gideon said unto God, Let not thine anger be hot against me, and I will speak but this once: let me prove, I pray thee, but this once with the fleece; let it now be dry only upon the fleece, and upon all the ground let there be dew.*
>
> *And God did so that night: for it was dry upon the fleece only, and there was dew on all the ground."*

JUDGES 6:36–40

Could God readily identify with Gideon's spiritual inaptitude?

Absolutely!

Did he accommodate Samuel's inexperience at his call?

Certainly!

Did He listen to Jeremiah's childish, quivering lips pouring out excuse at his calling?

Yes, He did!

Friend, your inexperience, inaptitude or lack of formal learning will *not* stop God from choosing, ordaining and anointing you for what purpose(s) you were created. This fact should put your mind at rest.

God will rise to your level of trust in order that He may lift you up to His level of faith. To do this, He does require, however, *your* availability and willingness to learn of Him. In all honesty, He requests your availability more than your ability.

Yes, He endowed you with those wonderful abilities and talents, but He alone reserves the understanding of *how*, *where* and *when* He would best channel those potentials within you so as to yield optimum returns. However, God cannot do a *thing* without your willingness and submissiveness coupled with a pure heart.

Your duty it is to seek the Father's face to receive the answers to the *how*, *when* and *where* questions I have earlier raised. Do not forget to clarify before the Lord what your specific *gifting* is! For instance, if you are called to preach, you must clarify before the Father, what exactly, your *specific message* is, so that you may *"give thyself wholly"* unto it; *"that thy profiting may appear to all."* [18]

Often times, God would train people practically, on the job. But because each battle requires different battle strategies, God may choose for you to learn through apprenticeship and mentoring, or request that you attend a formal education later in life!

In today's ever evolving scope of undertakings, we must take heed ensuring that we become relevant. Simply, the reason is because today's successful strategy may *not* work tomorrow. Whatever training/equipping route we agree to take, the underlying factor must be that of a willing, submissive protégé, ready to develop Heaven's downpayment of talents and abilities buried deep within their fabrics. So we would just present ourselves before God – with open, sincere hearts. When we have done this, Heaven's recommendation will then necessarily follow.

There is no *shunting* of God's rail-tracks. As Dr. Mike Murdock of The Wisdom Center, Texas, U.S.A once said: *"You can only be promoted by him from whom you took orders."*

The question then is, from whom do you take orders? Whose protégé are you?

In 1 Samuel 3:7, God by-passed the ninety-eight year

old, groggy, experienced Prophet Eli who had grown dismally nonchalant to the things of the Spirit for a three year old *'greenhorn'* who had what it takes to take over! Despite his inexperience to clearly understand the Lord's voice, Child Samuel was a budding candidate for God's use. While Eli – and his sons – had continuously grieved the Holy Spirit, Samuel was sensitive to the Spirit. One thing he knew very well to do, and that was to tarry in God's presence. That lone *know how* complemented for his inexperience. What a solace for those who do not have a formal education pathway to ministry-formation.

And whilst the backslidden old prophet went home to rest, Samuel rose to zest. The *'lil' chap'* learned to minister unto the Lord in the Temple in the *wee* hours of the morning when Eli's rest was transpiring into a deep sleep and a spiritual slumber. Shiloh's temple had become little Samuel's usual abode; the *watches* of the night, *his* times for spiritual alertness and watchfulness.

> *"And ere the lamp of God went out in the temple of the LORD, where the ark of God was, and Samuel was laid down to sleep."*

1 SAMUEL 3:3

Eli's ministerial experience would never again benefit him – nor his entire lineage, but his *very* replacement! The experience of the older is meant to be shoulders upon which the younger mounts into an unrestricted view-sight. The wisdom of the *older* minister therefore ought not to be lightly esteemed by the *younger!*

Gideon's fleece

Our text still dwells upon Judges 6:36–40.

Obliging Gideon through his fleece test requests was one of the sovereign acts of the Lord in the old dispensation that may *not* be re-enacted in the new, better dispensation of grace which we currently enjoy. Today, we have *"obtained a more excellent ministry ... established upon better promises."* [19]

Under the better dispensation of the New Testament, God expects us to *take Him at His word*. Nothing else. Nothing less! [20]

Simply, putting out fleeces before coming to terms with God is not a spiritual adept way of ascertaining God's perfect will for our lives. This following true story vividly illustrates my conviction even though identities have been altered to guarantee privacy.

Newlywed Julie is a beautiful, supposedly *born-again* Christian lady, from an impoverished African background, who was privileged to have been born in the United States of America. This legitimately entitles her to an American citizenship.

Here is her story. Her parents had moved back to Mother Africa once they had accomplished their feat in the Diaspora, in the early seventies. That was before Julie was ten. She'd felt 'torn away' from her friends and schoolmates; this deed actually became a source of unhappiness to her.

As she grew up, her father moved in between jobs and could hardly sustain his family. Julie's mom was training to be a professional. Money was hard to come by. Extended family members also were embittered that Julie's parents had not brought lasting gifts for them from the *'white-man's land!'*

An emerging teenager, Julie's unhappiness at school, discontent with an 'alien culture' – and the rejection she suffered from schoolmates because of her accent eventually started growing into a root of bitterness, deep within her.

She loathed her dad's strict disciplinary measures as a catholic gentleman to curtail her excesses and teenage rebellion. She managed to complete the basic final year GSCE examination, but with only two or three passes.

Julie's only burning desire was to travel back to the States and start a new life. However, her appeals fell on deaf ears: the relationship between herself and her father, further strained!

She ran away from home for the bright lights in the capital city on more than a few occasions. Julie partied and had sought for love and acceptance in the wrong quarters. Each of these encounters – at least with three different successive, very much older men – ended in pregnancies which she was unready to nurture. She aborted them in turns, under the most gruesome circumstances! (When she told me this part of her life's story; she was noticed to flinch, and a teardrop caressed each of her cheeks!)

Now in her mid-twenties, she rejected her Catholic upbringing for the Pentecostal setting. Here, she started attending church services – was reportedly converted – but was not *settled in* to absorb the rudiments of the *new birth*. Changes in her work places often mandated her change of worship venues.

A decade later, she married a man of her choice – nine months younger than she – with a joint understanding that she would travel out first and the husband would join later, because of his new work commitments. How they would raise the six digit ticket-fare however, was an enigmatic source of concern to them. The compulsory adjustments of a new home only climaxed her sincere desire to immigrate back to the States in order to *"help better our financial earnings as a couple"* – more so that economic conditions in this African state were fast deteriorating. These were her most sincere thoughts!

Many days, she and her sole-proprietor estate agent husband set aside days to honestly seek the face of the Lord for His direction.

Clearly, the Lord revealed unto them that there was going to be a woman's offer they must *not* accept. True to the word of the Lord, after a few months had elapsed, the woman's willingness "to help Julie" came aboard Julie's reach, first, through her erstwhile concerned Mom.

The *helper* woman was supposed to be a 'business lady.'

In an agreement secretly entered into by Julie and her mother, the *'business lady'* would loan Julie the ticket fare and arrange for her a room in her house, for the few weeks of her stay there! Julie had no foresight into the *collar chain* she was willing to wear.

Once a captive to this divisive lady, Julie could not clearly open up to her husband. Hidden to Julie and her Mom was the *'business lady's'* secret code to sex-trade Julie – and use her US citizenship to enforce illegal marriages with three different other men dangling out there between the crocodile-toothed American Immigration and Naturalization Service *(INS)* and the shameful shores of their respective countries of origin.

Unrevealed to any, money had exchanged hands between the *business-lady* and these men. Shambolic marriage dates had already been fixed for the remotest places in the U.S.

The broad-chested young men waited for their lucky breaks.

Back in Africa, Julie's travel date too was fixed for October 17th, 1997. Weeks transpired into mere days.

How would Julie now hatch her plot to her husband, barely two days to her departure for the United States?

She put out two fleeces to the Lord, a kitchen knife in her hand! *"Father"*, she moaned, *"if only honey wouldn't arrive by 6 pm Friday, October 17th; and if only this knife would strike the floor with its tip when I throw it up Lord, then I would believe this is your open door for us.''*

I could almost imagine your consternation. Or roar of laughter!

Anyway, the knife landed safely, on its side. But Julie's husband kept long hours at work that same day having had to seek after a defaulting tenant owing a large sum of money – which he had secretly planned to surprise Julie with, as his contribution towards her eternal longing!

Julie, glad for *answered prayers* hurriedly packed a few essentials into her tiny handbag. She was magnanimous enough to leave 'hubby' a hurriedly scribbled note, explaining her need to get to the capital city for some sum of money. She had thrown him this *red herring* of a close friend of hers who had promised to loan her some money towards her travel.

She vanished into thin air.

Julie had hoped to land in America – and give her husband a surprise call of *'answered prayers.'* Instead, she arrived at what was to become three months of unpleasant surprises. As soon as she had been seen past the immigration post, the *'business lady'* acted business-like: she took possession of Julie's passport; but Julie was unsuspecting.

In actuality, this shrewd businesswoman was a 'trafficker'; her field of expertise being *trafficking* immigration papers and arranging shambolic marriages between desperate men and women in Europe and the United States.

That was how she primarily earned her living, even though she had some other legitimate investments and business interests to divert government's attention off her shady dealings!

Julie emerged with gory tales. She was abused, brutalized and battered by the sex-trafficker lady and the different men *'arranged'* for her. Her indebtedness to them became quadrupled. She couldn't enforce any legal actions against her abusers. Her emotions were *yo-yo* like!

Julie's marriage – at that time, spared of collapse only by an escape as wide as an hair's-breadth's from colliding with hell's intents – would only last a decade! She was eventually divorced by her husband for marital infidelity and the gory, physical and violent abuses she had meted out on him!

Julie paid the price! But so also did her 'hubby' – and worse still, their innocent children!

She agrees today, in retrospect, that the price she'd paid – and is still paying –for her spiritual inaptitude, manipulative motives and utter insincerity are way too dear for *any* rational being to pay!

Chapter 5

Just Obey!

"To obey is better than sacrifice, and to hearken than the fat of rams."

- PROPHET SAMUEL

This chapter's title sounds rather militaristic: *Just Obey!* The reason I have designated it as such isn't far fetched. It may startle you, but it is nevertheless a fact: God is not a democrat! He does not await the result of either a referendum or a general consensus before commanding the action that puts into effect, your blessings. What God often does is advise you on the best course of action – and expect your compliance without complaints.

"I call heaven and earth to witness this day against you that I have set before you life and death, the

> *blessings and the curses; therefore choose life, that*
> *you and your descendants may live."* [1]

If we reject His advice and choose to rebel – as we had sometimes done in the past – we automatically experience in-built hardships that are as a result of our foolish choices! Some of us won't learn *doctrine* because we chose to rather learn by experience, which is more often than not, a harder teacher.

But isn't this what Christian growth entails: God's respect of our free will to moralize or justify our obedience or disobedience to Him?

> *"If they obey and serve him, they shall spend their*
> *days in prosperity, and their years in pleasures."*

JOB 36:11

The Amplified Version translates "pleasures" as *"pleasantness and joy."* In other words, God says: "If you listen to my pieces of advice and do them, you will spend all your days in good success and pros-perity – having no fear of lack or want – and in pleasantness and joy! That would be just like My Heaven on earth. That was – and still is – my original intent for you!"

> *"But if they obey not, they shall perish by the*
> *sword, and they shall die without knowledge."*

JOB 36:12

God warned the Israelites through Moses, as He does, us today:

"See, I have set before you this day and good, and death and evil.

[If you obey the commandments of the Lord your God which] I command you today, to love the Lord your God, to walk in His ways, and to keep His commandments and His statutes and His ordinances, then you shall live and multiply, and the Lord your God will bless you in the land …

But if your [mind and] heart turn away and you will not hear, but are drawn away to worship other gods and serve them,

I declare to you this day that you shall surely perish …"

DEUTERONOMY 30:15-18

If christian growth entails confronting the reality of the consequences of our choices made in light of our inability to rein down on our freewill, victorious Christian living however is summarized in just one word: *discipline!* Apostle Paul's apt summary best fits our description of a victorious Christian life. He describes how he daily attained this victory: *"I buffet my body [handle it roughly, discipline it by hardships] and subdue it"* to the obedience of Christ Jesus! [2]

We all want the peace of mind; and rightly so! The mind is the essential place from which peace must begin. And not until we've secured and anchored peace within our minds would we be able to extend it to another. But hardly do most realize that peace of mind commences with making peace *with* God!

The name *Jehovah Shalom* meaning *"The Lord my peace"* has its deep roots in commanding absolute obedience. Gideon's complete abandonment to God's specific instructions gave birth to that name *Jehovah Shalom!*

> *"And the LORD said unto him, Surely I will be with thee, and thou shalt smite the Midianites as one man.*
>
> *And he said unto him, If now I have found grace in thy sight, then show me a sign that thou talkest with me.*
>
> *Depart not hence, I pray thee, until I come unto thee, and bring forth my present, and set it before thee. And he said, I will tarry until thou come again.*
>
> *And Gideon went in, and made ready a kid, and unleavened cakes of an ephah of flour: the flesh he put in a basket, and he put the broth in a pot, and brought it out unto him under the oak, and presented it.*
>
> *And the angel of God said unto him, Take the flesh and the unleavened cakes, and lay them upon this rock, and pour out the broth. And he did so.*
>
> *And the angel of the LORD out forth the end of the staff that was in his hand, and touched the flesh and the unleavened cakes; and there rose up fire out of the rock, and consumed the flesh and the*

unleavened cakes. Then the angel of the LORD departed out of his sight.

And when Gideon perceived that he was an angel of the LORD, Gideon said, Alas, O Lord GOD! for because I have seen an angel of the LORD face to face.

And the LORD said unto him, Peace be unto thee; fear not: thou shalt not die.

Then Gideon built an altar there unto the LORD, and called it Jehovah Shalom: unto this day it is yet in Ophrah of the Abiezrites."

JUDGES 6:16–24

Notice, before Gideon's token offering could become acceptable to the Angel of the Lord, Gideon must first be purged!

Gideon, excited, asked the 'man' to wait for him while he hurried onto the business of preparing and fetching *his* token or present with which he would entertain his surprise guest! The Angel said that he would wait – and he awaited Gideon's return!

All well and good, set and ready. Gideon presented his gift to the Angel. But wait! Something is amiss.

The Angel showed Gideon the only way his present would be acceptable.

His first instruction was for Gideon to *"take the flesh"*; representing *his* worldly desires!

Next, the *"unleavened cakes"* – symbolizing sanctity and holiness. Finally, he was told to *"pour out the broth."* In other words, 'don't engage the broth on the offering.'

Do you know why?

It was because the broth was cooked in swine's flesh and other abominable things. The broth would represent Gideon's personal secret sins. (Please read Isaiah 65:2-4, for a fuller understanding).

David prayed for cleansing from secret and presumptuous sins. *"Cleanse thou me from secret faults. Keep back thy servant also from presumptuous sins; let them not have dominion over me: then shall I be upright, and I shall be innocent from the great transgression"* (Psalms 19:12).

Is the enemy – or an affliction – having the upper hand over you?

You too ought to pour out the broth!

Don't offer any sacrifice unto the Lord in the flesh. Keep your dough unleavened; neither pour Him the broth. The reason God has not been able to avenge you of *'the troubler'* up until now cannot be farfetched from your setting light His commandment. Otherwise, He is ready *"to revenge all disobedience, when your obedience is fulfilled."* [3]

Like the Angel waited for Gideon return, God's Father Heart waits! His heart yearns and longs for His chosen, silly, disobedient, willful children. Because of this, He shouts His loudest as to enforce their compliance to His instructions. At times like this, He *does* permit the introduction of some sort of suffering into these lives – with the assurance and expectation of their turning to Him, in their troubles! We ultimately defeat God's purpose if all we do is sulk, moan and turn *away from Him*, instead of *turning to Him*.

A Word on Obedience

Obedience is not what can be fully taught and grasped in the classroom. It is a practical subject; it emanates from deep within us, involving both the *intent* and *content* states of our hearts. We choose to obey God from the heart.

> *"For it is God which worketh in you, both to will and to do of his good pleasure."*

> PHILIPPIANS 1:13

God works *in* us. In other words, He – through His Holy Spirit – energizes and creates in us the power and desire to do His delight (*Amplified rendition*).

What is God's delight?

Jesus taught the disciples to pray: *"Thy will be done on earth, as it is in Heaven!"* [4] He availed us the summary of His earthly visit: *"Lo, I have come in the volume of the book to do your will, O, Lord."* [5] What delights God's heart as seeing His will executed on the earth – and in the lives of His children?

God's Spirit daily counts on and awaits your co-operation with His Spirit to execute and establish His will in your sphere of domain! You see, to choose to obey God, is to practice wisdom. To do otherwise is utmost folly!

Obedience and the Examiners' Tests

Your obedience cannot be fully measured without exposure to "spiritual examiners" just as a student's ability cannot be thoroughly evaluated except through the lenses of external examiners!

Now, I must clarify that there are two sources of spiritual examiners; each, having clearly different motives!

One *examiner* is God, Who *tests* us to better, perfect, and bring us to a state of showy display, as does a master craftsman. The other *examiner* is the devil; he *tempts* us with a sole diabolical purpose: expose our weaknesses so as to ridicule us with guilt, defeat and shame!

Even our Lord Jesus was not immunized against the devil's ploy:

"Who in the days of his flesh, when he had offered up prayers and supplications with strong crying and tears unto him that was able to save him from death, and was heard in that he feared;

Though he were a Son, yet learned he obedience by the things which he suffered;

Just Obey!

And being made perfect, he became the author of eternal salvation unto all them that obey him."

HEBREWS 5:7-9

Question: *How did Jesus our Lord learn obedience?*

Jesus learned obedience to His Father through offering up prayers to Him *in* the things He suffered! In today's plain language, we would render that verse above as: *"Jesus learned complete yielding to His Father's will by going through and praying through stuff!"*

Now, what 'stuff' are you going through that seems to outweigh you?

Master Jesus went through 'stuff' for a world of wild sinners – and He came out on the other side, triumphant. That gives me hope that *you*, too, will emerge victorious. Halleluyah!

This *suffering* eventually weakens the flesh until it's deadened, thus flagging off the commencement of the process of our perfection. Hebrews 2:9-10 reveals how Jesus became perfect in the days of His humanity:

> *"But we see Jesus, who was made a little lower than the angels for the suffering of death, crowned with glory and honor; that he by the grace of God should taste death for every man.*
>
> *For it became him, for whom are all things, and by whom are all things, in bringing many sons unto glory, to make the captain of their salvation perfect through sufferings."*

Your Double Nature

As evident in Gideon, there are two natures in *any* child of God: the flesh and the Spirit. And be not deceived, both are alive in him! However, the healthy child of God is willing to *kill* the flesh through the help of the Holy Spirit.

You mortify fleshly desires by a very conscious will. It is needful that you exercise domain over the flesh and its lustful passions.

How?

By willful starvation and deprivation! (We have conceived earlier, Apostle Paul's concept of how to achieve and maintain a victorious christian living.) You consciously and willingly starve to death, the fleshy tendencies while setting the spirit of your mind in an *ever-renewal* mode. [6]

The *spirit of our minds* works like the cruise control instrument in a car. Once set, it *is* set. No variance can disannul that setting.

I am sure you have set the *spirit of your mind* some-time in the past without you recognizing it. Let me give you an instance. When you vocalized a state-ment such as *'My mind is made up'* – and truly fol-lowed through on that which your mind was made up on or against; it was the *spirit of your mind* you had activated. This activation works in the negative as well as in the positive.

Active warring against the flesh entails *the* conscious effort on our part, setting that vital instrument – *the spirit of our minds* – against activities the Bible describes as "fleshly." There's no one who ever succeeded in life without achieving mastery over the *spirit of their minds*!

Life's battles and victories are fought and won in the mind. This is how you win, for instance, the battle over *any* addictions – or *excesses.* All addictive behaviors are rooted in selfish, fleshly, lustful passions.

In a matter as practical as shedding some excess pounds of flesh, for instance, you'd need to set the *spirit of your mind* on doing just that! You would watch your diet, hit the roads or use the gym.

You would win the battle over spiritual slothfulness by setting both the *spirit of your mind* and the alarm clocks to wake you up so you can meet the Father at certain early hours of the day to pray and study His Word. Mastery over spiritual matters to master the physical requires *hard* work and discipline, for it is the *spiritual* that controls the *physical*!

In Galatians 5:17, Apostle Paul establishes the fact that there is such a magnitude of unquantifiable strife in the spirit realm between the two natures in a newly born, growing or maturing christian:

> *"For the flesh lusteth against the Spirit, and the Spirit against the flesh: and these are contrary the one to the other: so that ye cannot do the things that ye would."*

But as *you* consciously continually wage this spiritual war in the arena of the mind, you will experience the flesh being gradually overpowered by the Spirit. It will become weaker, weakened – until it is dead! Mastery-over-the-flesh junction is a major junction God awaits each of His children, that He may commend them as His more-than-conqueror *sons* to the angels, the devil and the world!

> *"For if ye live after the flesh, ye shall die: but if ye through the Spirit do mortify the deeds of the body, ye shall live.*
>
> *For as many as are led by the Spirit of God, they are the sons of God."*

> ROMANS 8:13–14

You *must* start this conscious war over the flesh today. If you do, you would become spiritual and more accessible to things of the Spirit. Do not pardon or excuse the flesh and its lusts any further. Do not condone it turning you into an enemy of God.

> *"For to be carnally minded is death; but to be spiritually minded is life and peace."*

> ROMANS 8:6

Implicit and Explicit Disobedience

All through the scriptures, we find examples of implicit and explicit disobedience. The latter is the total disregard of the law or the deeds of the covenant. It is called outright rebellion. The implicit form of disobedience however, is also called *partial obedience.*

Whether partial or outright disobedience, disobedience of whatever form is deemed as rebellion in the eyes of God.

When God asked Saul to annihilate the Amalekites as their reward for ambushing in the desert the slaves redeemed from Egypt *en route* Canaan, Saul exhibited an implicit disobedience by sparing King Agag and saving the best of the sheep, oxen, lambs – *"and all that was good."* [7] Everything else that was ugly and vile, Saul indeed destroyed. God rejected him from being king, the day following.

Fleshly lusts do not have to be only sexual or sensualistic in orientation. Fleshly lusts could still find expressions through other avenues of our lives as lust of the eyes *(materialism)* or the pride of life *(egotism).* For instance, speaking roughly to an employee who is defenseless would, by biblical definitions, be fleshly. Your refusal to join a department in the House of God, to put to use your talents could be due to pride. But a conscious war must be waged against the flesh.

Now if the flesh dares catch a glimpse of warfare preparation ready to be waged against it by you, the next route option it will avail you is that of partial obedience.

Implicit disobedience is a way to a quick, irreparable loss because it has a tendency to cushion your conscience, thus rendering it hard. For example, if you have been struggling with co-habiting and fornicating – that is having sexual relationship with your boy/girlfriend without being married to them; flesh will concur to your initial reaction after having read a message as this, to ask them to leave the house.

It will then bid its time.

It will wait for your instincts and hunger to kick back at you! Soon, you find yourself at an agreed future date at a more 'exclusive' venue, with the promise of continued kissing – and possibly petting.

'But, at least, we haven't had sex ever since I asked him to move out', you'd soon find yourself reasoning!

Soon, your next date would be at a friend's self-contained apartment – who has gone to London for the weekend but has lent your boyfriend his keys! Gutted reaction greets you; you now seem weak against *your* flesh, *your* hunger and *your* desires!

In Revelation 3:15–16, God warned the lukewarm Laodicean christians:

> *"I know thy works, that thou art neither cold nor hot: I would thou wert cold or hot. So then because thou art lukewarm, and neither cold nor hot I will spue thee out of my mouth."*

Implicit obedience, at the start, may look insidious and harmless. For example, God explicitly called Abram out of his family background and country to a land He would show him:

Just Obey!

"Now the LORD had said unto Abram, Get thee out of thy country, and from thy kindred, and from thy father's house unto a land that I will shew thee."

G<small>ENESIS</small> 12:1

Did Abram obey?

Of course, he *did*. Only partially. Abram took Lot along with him.

"So Abram departed, as the LORD had spoken unto him; and Lot went with him ...

And Abram took Sarai his wife, and Lot his brother's son, and all their substance that they had gathered, and the souls that they had gotten in Haran; and they went forth to go into the land of Canaan; and into the land of Canaan they came."

G<small>ENESIS</small> 12:4–5

In the process of time, because of Abram, God was obliged to prosper Lot too. But Lot grew more aggressive and envious of Abram that there were open, deep grudges and resentments recorded between his men and Abram's servants.

Nephew Lot constituted a lot of hindrances to Abram's expansion. He dictated to and lorded over his Uncle's enterprises until the day Abram mustered enough strength to separate from him.

Even in the separation bid, Abram had to give preference to Lot above himself in the choice of settlement location. Covetous fleshly Lot chose the lush, well watered green plains of Jordan and left Abram with the option of the bare, rugged terrains.

Abram had learned the hard way.

Lot, however, had begun a disintegrating descent in the valley of Zoar. We were informed of this because Genesis 19:1 discloses that Lot's face had been rubbed in the sand! He sat defeated and lonely *"in the gate of Sodom."*

For Abram however, those high, rough terrains would soon translate into the culmination of a divine purpose: they would provide him an uninhibited panoramic view of Canaan, the Land God had promised him!

> *"And the LORD said unto Abram after that Lot was separated from him, Lift up now thine eyes, and look from the place where thou art northward, and southward, and eastward, and westward:*
>
> *For all the land which thou seest, to thee will I give it, and to thy seed for ever.*
>
> *And I will make thy seed as the dust of the earth: so that if a man can number the dust of the earth, then shall thy seed also be numbered."*

GENESIS 13:14–16

Separation from Lot afforded Abram the opportunity not only of sight, but also of hearing. He heard the

Lord re-commit Himself to delivering unto him, the exact geographical boundaries of his *portion*. Yes, there is an exact *portion* of inheritance to each of God's children. Only an unrivaled obedience to the Father in yielding to His perfect will will guarantee *their* possession of it!

Obey the Lord in running your finances. Follow His guidelines outlined in His will, His Word! Be prudent. God demands our explicit, total obedience that we release *all* our tithes to Him as a *'premium cover'* on the covenant He shares with us. Notice, I have chosen to use the word *cover* – because when you purchase an insurance premium, your timely monthly re-payments ensure the continuity of your insurance premium. It indemnifies you against the purposes for which cover was sought.

In the same way, your tithe is your *payback* over God's covenant of covering upon your life. You are not doing God a favor by paying back on this divine premium. Bringing in anything lesser than the wholesome 10% of your earnings and profit is an example of implicit disobedience. Even ministers of the gospel also are not exempt from tithe-payments.

We read of God's irrevocable unequivocal plan of financial freedom for His children:

> *"Will a man rob God? Yet ye have robbed me. But ye say, Wherein have we robbed thee? In tithes and offerings.*

Bring ye all the tithes into the storehouse, that there may be meat in mine house, and prove me now herewith, saith the LORD of hosts, if I will not open you the windows of heaven, and pour you out a blessing, that there shall not be room enough to receive it.

And I will rebuke the devourer for your sakes, and he shall not destroy the fruits of your ground; neither shall your vine cast her fruit before the time in field, saith the LORD of hosts.

And all nations shall call you blessed: for ye shall be a delightsome land, saith the LORD of hosts."

MALACHI 3:8, 10–12

What about your vows?

Vows are a test of man's integrity, proving the sincerity of his avowed speech. [8] When your hands cannot be trusted to fulfill that which your mouth has uttered in love, something must be drastically wrong with that heart from which that vow has been made.

When you defer to pay that which you have vowed, God calls you a "fool" (or for more modern translation, a "rebel").

In Ecclesiastes 5:4 we read:

"When thou vowest a vow unto God, defer not to pay it; for He hath no pleasure in fools: pay that which thou hast vowed."

God sees a willful deferment redeeming your vow as an affront on His Word; potentially, a locking of horns of your personality with His! This rebellious act surely will pull the strings, tighter, on God's 'bags of pleasures' originally meant for you.

> *"Be it far from me; for them that honour me I will honour, and they that despise me shall be lightly esteemed."*

> 1 SAMUEL 2:30

Intentional negligence redeeming a vow disrupts heaven's economics of *supply* balancing *demand.* [9] Vow-neglect will certainly open the door to the devourer to systematically demolish whatever you are so concerned building up.

> *"Suffer not thy mouth to cause thy flesh to sin; neither say thou before the Angel, that it was an error: wherefore should God destroy the work of thine hands?"*

> ECCLESIASTES 5:6

Now, if your circumstances happened to have changed – between the time that you made your vow, and the present – so that you are now experiencing a tough challenge redeeming it; that would represent a different matter. Simply, you acknowledge your vow to God – and ask Him to make a way for you to redeem it, in good time. And He will!

We have been discussing a few of the commonest

types of *implicit* disobedience – and the repercussions that could result should you chose to continue indulging in such acts. Now, let me share with you a few instances of *explicit* disobedience.

Rebellion is the outright explicit disobedience to God's words. On the field of play of an *English Premiership*, an intentional foul play, a heartless conduct, a reckless physical or verbal charge at another with an intent to cause harm, breakage or damage calls for the referee's swift penalty and punishment. In like manner, under God's Word, rebellion attracts God's *hot* wrath.

Rebellion does not always need to be loud and rash; sometimes, it may be subtle, undermining, and cunningly-crafted! With reference to King Saul's audacious rebellion – recorded in 1 Samuel 15 which God hinted Prophet Samuel about in the middle of the very night – when asked why he had not destroyed Amalek utterly as God had commanded, but had brought along the sheep and oxen which were now bleating and lowing in the backside of the palace, Saul invented a lie. Obviously, this was a *cover-up* lie tied round an acceptable, excusable, godly reason!

> *"And Saul said unto Samuel, Yea, I have obeyed the voice of the LORD, and have gone the way which the LORD sent me, and have brought Agag the king of Amalek, and have utterly destroyed the Amalekites.*

But the people took of the spoil, sheep and oxen, the chief of the things which should have been utterly destroyed to sacrifice unto the LORD thy God in Gilgal."

1 SAMUEL 15:20–21

Saul had coyly interwoven a righteous act of service unto the Lord, with a wrong motive – and a wrong reason. How many of us have perfectly executed a righteous act, but with a wrong motive?

Recognizing a Rebellious heart

We recognize a rebellious heart because it does *not* repent when confronted. Instead, it invents polished excuses. It dives for a 'cover' in *kingly* robes, hoping to be spared.

A rebellious heart may also perhaps, once in a while, find appropriate *Kung-fu* robes if it felt never ever so cheated, hoping to self-defend.

On the contrary, a contrite spirit *feels* brokenness and emptiness! In the spirit realm, when we are at loggerheads with God's gentle Spirit, we'd definitely sense when that cord of treasured relationship with God, snaps! We'd lose all peace! Rather than cover up, a broken and contrite heart pleads for God's mercy.

God's preference reasons of David over Saul as king are very glaring. Despite the atrocious sins he committed against God, David was quick to acknowledge, repent and plead for God's mercy, once the understanding of his sin was made known to him. This was why in spite of the futuristic misdeeds he would commit once on the throne, God would still affirm David as *"a man after his heart."* [10]

Is God unfair?

No, not at all.

The reason for God's preference of David over Saul can best be summed up in the understanding David possessed. He was advantaged over Saul in that he had *the* understanding of an engaging, on-going, working relationship with the Spirit of God! A humble, contrite heart applies itself to understanding; David possessed the undergirding principle that *"the LORD seeth not as man seeth; for man looketh on the outward appearance, but the LORD looketh on the heart."* [11] What a lesson! The *"written off"* could soon be written upon! God judges us *not* based upon our outward conduct but the motives of our heart.

Once sin is confessed with a sincere repentant heart to God and the Blood of Jesus Christ, God's holy Son is appropriated; forgiveness and cleansing, restoration and healing are enforced. The holy heavenly God will never again remember such sins. He deems the guilty pardoned, ransomed, healed, restored, forgiven and guiltless. The rebellious, however, dwells in a *"dry land."* [12]

Saul's rebellion will not be pardoned, but speedily judged:

"And Samuel said, Hath the LORD as great delight in burnt offerings and sacrifices, as in obeying the voice of the Lord? Behold, to obey is better than sacrifice, and to hearken than the fat of rams.

For rebellion is as the sin of witchcraft, and stubbornness is as iniquity and idolatry. Because thou hast rejected the word of the LORD, he hath also rejected thee from being king."

1 SAMUEL 15:22–23

That was God's verdict! Saul's authority as king was suddenly expired!

"He, that being often reproved and hardeneth his neck, shall suddenly be destroyed, and that without remedy."

PROVERBS 29:1

From the daintiest, Saul began his spiral journey to the dingiest. The Word of God further warns that whoever covers his sin will not prosper, but he/she who confesses and renounces them shall have mercy:

"He that covereth his sins shall not prosper: but whoso confesseth and forsaketh them shall have mercy."

PROVERBS 28:13

Rebellion: an Attempt to Put into Disarray God's Universe Order-Framework

God's universe is governed by laws set up in hierarchical orders much like that displayed in grandfather clock which contains wheels within wheels, each turning the other to exact precision.

Orderliness births efficiency. To achieve a time-frame that is efficient, God set His laws in place. God's laws govern, on God's behalf, God's universe. Now, whenever any rebels against a godly instituted authority – whether implicitly or explicitly – such act is an aberration aimed at disenfranchising God's entire vast Universe. This is the mystery surrounding the sin of witchcraft: witches and the occult, in general, attempt to thwart by wrest and tussle, God's ordinations and timings.

> *"Rebellion is as the sin of witchcraft and stubbornness is as iniquity and idolatry."*

> 1 SAMUEL 15:23

Have you been practicing witchcraft, unbeknown to you?

Have you been a subject, dominated by witchcraft's manipulations of delays, denials and deceits?

I prophesy in the mighty name of Jesus, this day as your day of rejoicing. Your reading this book thus far demonstrates your quest for escape!

This is your way of escape, announced:

Just Obey!

"Let every soul be subject unto the higher powers. For there is no power but of God: the, powers that be are ordained of God.

Whosoever therefore resisteth the power; resisteth the ordinance of God: and they that resist shall receive to themselves damnation."

ROMANS 13:1–2

Please note, *God's ordained powers* could be the church, civil, matrimonial, parental, organizational – or indeed those of establishments. We are enjoined to *not* resist such powers or authorities set over us.

Our watchword is "resist" – and we need to have a firm grasp of it.

Collins Concise dictionary, defines the word "resist" as *"to stand firm against; not yield to; fight against, be proof against; to oppose; refuse to accept or comply with."* [13]

Authoritative powers are in place, for *your* protection. Opposing or resisting such godly mandates is simply submitting yourself under – and opening up your spirit unto – the spirit of witchcraft.

In Africa, Latin America and Asia where there is a generality of women being dominated by men which in itself is an abuse of culture; womenfolk generally have come to view rules set by men as oppressive. Housewives think they are curtailed. In their own eyes, they have become a *specie*, endangered! Some wives in the church, therefore, in trying to navigate around their husbands' stipulations end up manipulating their men. This bears terrible repercussions on the entire family.

Needless to say, these examples above are a few instances of the demonstration of the spirit of opposition, resistance or witchcraft! This witchcraft type does not necessarily have to be airborne; all required is just a little rebellion – just a little resistance, just a little opposition, just a little disobedience. Rebellion is the spirit *"according to the course of this world, according to the prince of the power of the air (Satan), the spirit that now worketh in the children of disobedience."* [14]

Disobedience of any sort to godly rules makes us automatically become children of disobedience. We readily become access victims to the merciless devil and his demons. Hence, to block Satan's inflow into our lives, God instituted ordinances and laws which are expected to guide our human conduct. Your liberation is encapsulated in obeying without questioning, God's authority set over you.

God's ordinance of balance for example, in matrimonial relationship is found in the man and the woman conducting themselves and deferring unto each other, out of reverence for God. [15]

Furthermore, we are enjoined:

> *Wives, submit yourselves unto your own husbands, as unto the Lord.*

For the husband is the head of the wife; even as Christ is the head of the church: and he is the saviour of the body.

Therefore as the church is subject unto Christ, so let the wives be to their own husbands, in everything.

*Husbands, **love your wives**, even as Christ also loved the church, and gave himself for it."*

(EPHESIANS 5:22–25; EMPHASIS, MINE)

God's Specific Command to Gideon

God's specific command to Gideon was recorded in Judges 6:25–26:

"And it came to pass the same night, that the LORD said unto him, Take thy father's young bullock, even the second bullock of seven years old, and throw down the altar of Baal that thy father hath, and cut down the grove that is by it:

And build an altar unto the LORD thy God upon the top of this rock, in the ordered place, and take the second bullock, and offer a burnt sacrifice with the wood of the grove which thou shalt cut down."

Gideon's execution of God's order, unlike King Saul's, was perfect in all ramifications. For his obedience, God commended Gideon – and stood by him. Gideon's fearful, timid nature was complemented by God's enablement, which became a source of strength to him. Being of a sincere heart, he could not muster the boldness to destroy Baal's altar in broad daylight, so *"he did it by night."* [16] How God trains His Generals!

The thick darkness of the night time was just transpiring into dawn! The whole city awoke to discover a mishap had befallen their idol, its altar and the grove. Uproar began. To uncover the culprit, they would cast lots.

The lots fell on Gideon.

When his father Joash was summoned to the city center, they demanded that his son pay the ultimate price for his audacity in destroying their god – and its altar! But the only one and true living God gave the father quick wisdom which eventually saved Gideon's life:

"And Joash said unto all that stood against him, will ye plead for Baal? Will ye save him? ... if he be a god, let him plead for himself, because one hath cast down his altar."

JUDGES 6:31

Friends, such protection, breakthrough and favor attend an obedient person. If you would dare obey Him from your heart, unquestionably, God promises to take care of all the troubles that you would encounter. He'd go ahead of you and waive all evil counsels fore-determined against you. Obedience pays.

Now, God's command to Gideon – as evident in the verse, was four-fold:

1 *Take thy father's young bullock – (and) even the seven year old bull ...,*
2 *Overthrow the altar of Baal that thy father hath,*
3 *Cut down the grove that is by it, and;*
4 *Build another altar to the LORD the God!*

Let us examine them, each briefly.

1. Take the Bulls ...

> *"And it came to pass the same night, that the LORD said unto him, Take thy father's young bullock, even the second bullock of seven years old ..."*

Notice with me God's request to Gideon to sacrifice two bulls: first; a tender bullock – then, the older, seven year old bull.

First, God would demand an atoning sacrifice – in the form of the sacrifice of this young bullock – for the outward, more visible personal weaknesses, flaws – or indeed sins of Gideon, lest his mission to deliver Israel from the Midianites become jeopardized! **God's logical sequence of atonement still is that only after the** *deliverer's* **personal sins have been atoned for, could he become qualified to deliver others!**

In another spiritual translation of God's demand,

doesn't it sound like Jesus' teaching of first removing the mote in your eye, before attempting to remove the beam from some else's eye? [17]

Second, God's command to Gideon was to also offer in sacrifice, the older bull.

Of what significance could this be?

Now, because of their indefatigable raw strength, bulls, in spiritual terms represent demonic influences. Sacrificing this older bull could mean God saying to you to be mindful of – and take down – demonic footholds or strongholds! He commanded Gideon to *"take it"*. In other words, *"arrest, seize by force, the demonic foothold or stronghold in the city."*

Footholds are like ledges on a steep rock, or like a ridge of rock lying beneath the surface of a sea. Ledges protruding from a wall or a window provide a thief an opportuned leverage to burgle a house. Ledges under the sea could be fatal to an unwary sailor!

A demonic foothold may be as innocuous as an age-long superstitious belief in a people; a belief which antagonizes the Word of the Lord! It could just be the plain TV or the Computer screen you burn hours on end before, starring at! You watch unedifying news, talk-show programs – and just, plain 'old' junk!

Do you realize that it has been proven that people could become addicted to computer games?

Another *ledge* could be that friend of yours from

youth, who, however refuses to submit his/her life to Christ's rule; yet wields so great influence on your personality!

While spiritual ledges are insidious, strongholds are obtrusive. Strongholds usually are born in our minds as ledges; with inadequate attention being paid them, they soon protrude – and become noticeable! Take for instance; someone who always had believed all their life not to steal may suddenly be confronted by a crispy £20 note lying on a quiet street corner, gently blown by the wind! This 'believer' had looked both ways before reaching to the ground with their long fingers and pocketing the money! It could be that a reputable, highly respected family figure in the society has sacrificed hours watching pornography. The realization of his betrayal dawned on him *only* after he'd cheated on his wife of twenty-one years! Worse still, He couldn't believe *how it all started!* I'd tell you *how*: it all started as a quiet, insidious *ledge* that transformed into a stronghold.

Isn't that the natural course of progression into any addictive behavior?

Your stronghold could be disguised as an academic rejection of or mind attack on some teachings in God's Holy Word, the Bible. Still, the Holy Spirit whispers His loudest: *"take down this bull!"*

It's also interesting to note that we were informed of the age of the bull; it was *seven* years old!

Now, because you have read thus far, God may want

you *"to terminate by force; take authority over by seizure,"* a foothold or stronghold that has dominated your life, home or business, the past seven years! The number *seven* represents spiritual perfection; the end of an era!

Thus, I prophesy to you in the name of Jesus: "This day marks the end of the era of the reign of the wicked, demonic *bulls of Bashan*, in your life!" This freedom is yours for the taking, in Jesus' name; so, *"take it."* And by force!

2. Overthrow Baal's Altar

Far from popular conception, Joash, Gideon's father, was not a man of mere means. He was an influential man in Ophrah. He had single-handedly erected the altar of Baal in the city center, which had now become the god or the idol of the entire city. We see it clearly in the command of God to Gideon:

"… throw down the altar of Baal that thy father hath …"

What is an idol?

An idol could be a physical statue of a god, erected at an altar – or represented by a symbol. **The Bible however, defines an idol as** *"anything* **that dethrones God and is placed as a substitute in the place of God in the human heart."**

Baal worship was an idolatrous practice, forbidden by the God of Israel. Long before Israel entered the Promised Land, God had forewarned them in Deuteronomy 12:1–3:

> *"These are the statutes and judgments, which ye shall observe to do in the land, which the LORD God of thy fathers giveth thee to posses it, all the days that ye live upon the earth.*
>
> *Ye shall utterly destroy all the places, wherein the nations which ye shall possess served their gods, upon the high mountains, and upon the hills, and under every green tree:*
>
> *And ye shall overthrow their altars, and break their pillars and burn their groves with fire; and ye shall hew down the graven images of their gods, and destroy the names of them out of that place."*

Israel was forewarned against permissiveness and lawlessness, the very things they embraced.

In Deuteronomy 12:8 God had warned:

> *"Ye shall not do after all the things that we do here in the land this day, every man whatsoever is right in his own eyes."*

Family gods *do* exist! These 'gods' may have been passed down unto us, through the lineage.

For most people today, their job has become their god!

There could also be idolatrous practices we have witnessed our parents observe which had caused them, us – and many unsuspecting others, to err. As God's true child, you must ask for wisdom and strength to overthrow such gods, idolatrous acts or belief systems that had given rise to such altars or gateways into the demonic or the occult! *You* cleanse and rid your homes, families, work establishments and communities of demonic altars.

Yes, you have been admonished to *"obey your parents in the Lord."* [18] You are not in disobedience if you refuse to participate with parents in idolatry, idolatrous practices or disobedient acts that would ensnare your destiny and nip your potential in the bud!

Stop co-habiting with idols – whether in the literal or physical sense! *"There shall no strange god be in thee; neither shalt thou worship any strange god."* [19]

On June 5, 1982 a tragic irrecoverable incident befell our sister, twenty-two year old Joan. The family was never left the same, again! Joan was married and pregnant, but was unable to safely deliver after nine months. She needed to undergo a *caesarian*. However, it ended a botched op. Not only did the infant not survive, Joan also lost her life. She heaved her last breath in Mother's arms at the hospital! Mourners and sympathizers besieged our home in throngs – and it was the latter group who advised Mother to *wise up!* "Seek protection and be fortified, you and the other children", they enthused.

In no time, we were taken from a white garment false prophet to another. We encountered innumerable native witch-doctors. We were being *fortified!* So we thought, or were made to believe.

The devil would readily humiliate any idolater. We

were given to eat and lick all manner of powdered substances offered to demons. Foul smelling colored drinks were given to us to drink. We had been deluded to have descended so low. We almost even bordered on necromancy to help avenge our losses.

A third child of original four children, I was earlier than this time, a born again, tongue-speaking third-form *Scripture Union* member at secondary school; but I lacked the overpowering overwhelming mandate to effect any positive change in family affairs. My elder brother was not born again – and was soon traveled out of the country to pursue his education in Europe. My kid sister – at eight years of age – was too young to understand the spiritual implications of these gloomy clouds that hung over our family's history. Mom was a *shade* too broad to refuse. Dad was overpowered by this sad chapter in his family's experience – and though he objected to us children being subjected to these harrowing abuses, yet had no will power of his own to enforce a halt to Mother's spiritual *felonious* acts endorsed by her circle of influence.

I'd always loved Mother, but I was nonetheless very angry towards her at this time. I had only turned fourteen (earlier that March), and already possessed a mind of my own. I knew God loved me, but I was becoming rebellious even at Him! *How could God watch us go so low?* That thought pre-occupied me most days that evolved into weeks and later, months. I was confused about God's great unconditional love.

One thing I did in my pain: I had masterminded my anger toward the last witchdoctor. I had wished and prayed him evil over the ensuing weeks!

So on one of our visits to him again, I had lost my nerves and had let loose my *holy vent* on this demonic *medium*. I had pronounced a death sentence on him in the name of the Lord Jesus who saved me at three years of age! That day; at a sitting, as punishment, I was made to endure about a hundred lacerations on my head to cast out the supposed demon in me, which had emboldened me. (Don't yell at me at this disclosure, you or your lineage may not be that innocent afterall!)

True to the prophetic word, the witch doctor died within half a year!

But for years, we remained bound until the light of God's Word dawned upon us. This light enabled us to begin to seek more intensely, God's face, counsel, forgiveness and deliverance! Subsequently – almost a decade later or so – Mother herself became a genuine, born again christian. Unfortunately, up until now, my brother remains at large, away from the forgiveness and love the Lord offers!

You see, God's Word says: *"their sorrows shall be multiplied that hasten after another god."* Same holds true of co-habiting with or holding unto accursed items whether they be clothes, jewelries, money – or indeed capital assets bequeathed as inheritances. Read it for yourself in Psalms 16:4:

"Their sorrows shall be multiplied that hasten after another god: their drink offerings lifeblood will I not offer, nor take up their names into my lips."

What are you supposed to do with accursed inheritances?

You redeem them.

To redeem something means to buy it back from destruction. You redeem accursed items by submitting such into the hands of the Lord through a true minister of God who is empowered by heaven to reverse the curses.

In some cases, such inheritances or endowments are donated to the work of the Lord, or channeled into charities that relieve poverty, homelessness, starvation or natural disasters across the world. Some other instances would call for a physical bonfire being set to such bequeathed properties.

I do also strongly opine that any who had visited the mediums before or had incisions made on any part of their bodies seek thorough deliverance from the blood covenants contracted by them or on their behalf. Your denial of such blood covenants will not help in realizing your potentials. Your ignorance about blood covenants will not disconnect and dislodge the strongman and his activities. The truth is, the exchange of genotypic fluids with the demonic world is a sure avenue of initiating a body into – and introducing the many varied chronic bondages, illnesses, mysterious losses or prolonged delays to that person! Incisions enforce demonic covenants.

Only the renunciation of such covenants through the Blood of the Lamb will nullify every diabolical effects of initiated covenants. May your ignorance not compound your foolishness!

Apostle Paul in Romans 8:35, 37–39 inquires:

> *"Who shall separate us from the love of Christ? Shall tribulation, or distress, or persecution, or famine, or nakedness or peril, or sword?*
>
> *Nay, in all these things we are more than conquerors through him that loved us.*
>
> *For I am persuaded, that neither death, nor life, nor angels, nor principalities, nor powers, nor things present, nor things to come.*
>
> *Nor height, nor depth, nor any other creature, shall be able to separate us from the love of God, which is in Christ Jesus our Lord."*

Whatever trouble that does trouble you ought not to derail your faith in Christ. And honestly speaking, your particular *issue* cannot be an *issue* to the Almighty Father. The Scripture teaches:

> *"There hath no temptation taken you but such as is common to man: But God is faithful, who will not suffer you to be tempted above that ye are able; but will with the temptation also make a way to escape, that ye may be able to bear it."*

1 CORINTHIANS 10:13

God, in these last days, is entrusting the focus and emphasis of salvation of homes upon the children and the young adults therein, who know Him! Upon them He has placed His high expectation.

> *"I have written unto you, fathers, because ye have known him that is from the beginning. I have written unto you, young men, because ye are strong, and the word of God abideth in you, and ye have overcome the wicked one."*

1 JOHN 2:14

This is the *bridge-builder* generation. We shall remain focused, standing in the gaps created by our fore-runners: *"to the intent that now unto the principalities and powers in heavenly places might be known by the church the manifold wisdom of God."* [20]

Thus, all the gods and altars of ir-reverent practices and worship in our homes will be demolished! We wouldn't give the tiniest spec of a space to any ac-cursed thing – ever again!

One quick lesson we surely will draw out of Gideon being chosen as the right man for the job to uproot the altar of Baal is that, God commences His work, targeting the *bull's eye.* He knows that it is only by hampering the *bull* where it hurts, that would over-power it! My announcement from God is that He is now set to 'arrest' many a *bull's eyes* of family heads, rich, corporate, influential men and women of our time – and by so doing, save the very elect of our time, still out there dining at the devils' altars!

3. Cut down the Grove

"… and cut down the grove …"

This was God's third command to Gideon: *"cut down the grove …"*

Groves, in those times, were short canopy-forming trees with green leaves that produced plenty of shades and cover that shielded from the rays of the scorching sun. Not only were the green lush foliages of use as protection from the penetrating sun; they were more needed, in fact, for ensuring the privacy and secrecy of those who had visited Baal, and had sauntered into the pleasurable excesses of the worship of Ashtaroth. These groves, usually lined up adorably, in plantation-style, the surrounding areas of the altar of Baal.

The worship of Ashtaroth involved the practice of all manner of indecencies, lustful passions, immoralities and orgies. Her worship was superstitiously believed to stimulate rain, thus birthing the expectation of abundant harvests. This was the major reason the people invoked demon Ashtaroth at crops' seeding times, female animals' heat seasons and human fertility periods. Her effigies were made of wood spiritually connected with the groves of trees – though *her* demon is symbolized by a pole erected by the altar of Baal called Asherah pole.

The worship of Baal and Ashtaroth meant that the children of Israel were enslaved in the five existential realms of human endeavors *vis-à-vis* spiritual, financial, emotional, socio-relational and reproductive! What an enslavement lack of control of Man's appetites can cause! In another word, the next third to fourth generations of Israelites yet unborn had been enslaved: they had been automatically dedicated to demons Ashtoreth and Baal while their parents were conceiving them.

Yet, God's resounding command to Gideon was to *"cut down the grove."*

Some Examples of the Groves of our Time

These days, the use of the cyber-active highway plus its accessories like the *e-mail, e-Banking, Skype, Facebook, Twitter and* the *You-Tube* are all positive achievements for us as humans. We are all enriched by the technological advancements of this day and age.

But what happens when Man begins to make a god of his God-endowed creativity? As Prophet Isaiah had rightly noticed:

> *"Their land also is full of silver and gold, neither is there any end of their treasures; their land is also full of horses, neither is there any end of their chariots:*
>
> *Their land also is full of idols; they worship the work of their own hands, that which their own fingers have made."*

ISAIAH 2:7–8

Of course, when Man begins to worship his idealized creation, he automatically becomes a captive of his own witty inventions.

You roll off your bed early in the morning; but the first *thing* you do is *Tweet* the world via your Blackberry. For some, *FB* is their first port of call. The sanctity of the precious early moments of the day meant to be spent with the Lord in fellowship has been lost to gadgetry.

And you reckon that God will not be jealous for His holy name?

Our children log on-line very frequently to play games, chat with their friends and 'get' social. But so also do scammers, perverts and pedophiles, lurking around dark, *groovy* places, searching for avenues to fuel their lusts!

The fashion industry of today has transformed from early 90's *miniskirts* and 2000's *micro-mini's* into nudist public campaigns of 2010. I remember when we were growing up; we never saw so much *flesh* portrayed on national television just to advertise any product; let alone, ordinarily, a toothpaste brand! What we *grew up* viewing were models with perfect sets of white, healthy dentition – and pristine smiles to the envy of adoring little minds. (I still do wear a perfect healthy set of dentition anyone will be privileged to possess: thanks to those role-models of the late '60's!)

Don't fool yourselves, parents; the generality of your Christless youths are already emotionally and psychologically *burned* beyond otherwise could be perceived by you. Little surprise you witness from them such an aggressive and a flagrant flaunting of *everything* moral, ethical and spiritual: you have not visited their *groves*!

Today's modern society, at large, suffers from various new names of diseases and emotional traumas unheard of in our parents' generations. A few suffer, basically, from a root cause of low self-esteem or lack of a positive self accreditation. So, they for instance, dress to trap – and seduce. Some others eat to *die* – and die to eat. We dance to arouse – and are aroused by a *dance*. We lust to *love*, and love to lust! We work to drop – or *drop* working altogether!

Oh, that the Spirit of the Lord would swoop upon our land and heal our deathly hearts and minds.

But our responsibility it is to take a step in faith, obey the voice of the Lord crying out: *"Cut down the grove."*

Will you heed God's Spirit call to you today to destroy the hidden, dark, pleasure-yielding places of wickedness – wherever they may exist?

Tammy – not her real name – was a young born again Christian woman of marriageable age whose background I was privileged to know. She visited *my* office sometime ago. She was agitated when she suffered the sixth broken engagement in three years.

In a dramatic move, a friend overseas had helped her *"find"* a ready husband who had recently won the U.S.

Visa Lottery. The suitor was supposed to be a born-again christian from the *bondwoman's* religion; his immediate family members, are still neck-deep in it!

Tammy who looked so concerned asked of my opinion!

"Frankly, I have no opinion of my own" I retorted, taking a pause, to enable me reach for my Bible which was away at an arm's length. Hardly had I completed this half statement, than she heaved a deep breath. At this, the Lord revealed her heart's depth onto me. The Lord said to me: *She already has erected this newfound suitor's idol in her heart no matter what you counsel.* In other words, she has turned desperate – and was ready to "settle."

The Lord warned me of the imminent danger of being misquoted now or in the future in an attempt to battle for her soul, so I held my peace!

Should any who have pre-meditated the course of rebellion in their heart anymore demand of God the right way?

Ezekiel 14:3–5 answers aptly:

> *"Son of man, these men have set up their idols in their heart, and put the stumblingblock of their iniquity before their face: should I be enquired of at all by them?*

> *Therefore speak unto them, and say unto them, Thus saith the Lord GOD; Every man of the house of Israel that setteth up his idols in his heart and putteth the stumblingblock of his iniquity before his face, and cometh to the prophet; I the LORD*

will answer him, that cometh according to the multitude of his idols.

That I may take the house of Israel in their own heart, because they are all estranged from me through their idols."

Your case may not be exactly like Tammy's but would you want to heed the Spirit's bid from the heart?

Then listen: It is scripturally unsound for any man or woman to "find" a husband or wife for another even if they are within the same neighborhood; let alone overseas – and at that, strangers!

God has committed unto the male alone, that task of finding the *bone of his bones* – and possibly, his missing ribs! Please don't give a thought to the Agony Aunts on periodicals or *"internet personals"*; for instance, who suggest to the female, "Tips on How to Woo, Seduce and Win a Man's Approval." I have actually stumbled upon such sites that offer – what in their own un-refined opinion; they call – "candid words of advice on how to steal your best friend's man." You know that you're a child of God – and that God doesn't speak as in such terms!

So how does God speak?

God speaks mainly through His Word. So, God's word tells us in Proverbs 18:2: *"Whoso findeth a wife findeth a good thing and obtaineth the favour of the LORD."*

Moreover, God's command in Romans 14:5 counsels prospective *'go-betweens'* to totally relent their grips off their intended victims. *"Let every man be fully persuaded in his own mind"*, we were told!

In the same vein, an intending christian spinster ought to not ask for peoples' opinions about a christian bachelor who feels led of the Lord to ask for her hand in friendship that could lead to courtship and marriage. She should rather go seek the face of the Father in prayer. It ought not to be heard that she gives the bachelor's name to the spiritists to *help* inquire from mediums whether or not the intending suitor is the right partner for her!

The Master Shepherd assures *"he calls his own sheep by name and brings (leads) them out."* [21] We must individually learn to identify our Shepherd's still small voice!

Now, *go-between's* had been used in the dark ages to contract marriage proposals in some customs. These days of enlightenment; however, utmost premium must be placed on the mind of the bride-to-be. Eliezer, Abraham's eldest servant was an *authorized agent* to search for and fetch home Isaac's wife, Rebekah. By divine arrangement, the eligible lady was quickly found! Eliezer was a little overjoyed for answered prayers. He was thus, a bit impatient. He wanted to 'hush up' Rebekah's family that he be allowed to take her home to Abraham and Isaac. But Rebekah's parents and siblings needed to inquire first from their daughter and sister. Here is the account recorded for us in Genesis 24:56-59:

> *"And he said unto them, Hinder me not, seeing the LORD hath prospered my way; send me away that I may go to my master.*
>
> *And they said, We will call the damsel, and enquire at her mouth.*
>
> *And they called Rebekah, and said unto her, Wilt thou go with this man? And she said, I will go.*
>
> *And they sent away Rebekah their sister, and her nurse, and Abraham's servant, and his men."*

Here, Rebekah willingly consented to the marriage proposal contracted by Eliezer on behalf of his master Abraham's son, Isaac. If football or cricket match-fixing is an international crime, marital matchmaking must be a heinous crime!

Recent studies show in England that more than 20,000 young ladies of African, Asian, or Middle Eastern descent are forced into organized marriages even against their wishes yearly. [22]

This is an ungodly practice. Every man and woman must be allowed to be responsible for their choices in destiny.

And if you met over the internet, please take sufficient amount of time to understudy the potential mate. You commence your 'understudy', first, by e-mail correspondence! This could be possibly followed by telephone call conversations over a suitable length of time before committing to meet them in person.

When agreeing to meeting, please arrange to meet at public places in the company of one or two trusted friends. Never agree to meet a *stranger* in secluded places or in privacy.

Allow parents – and more than three core friends of yours to know of your intent and whereabouts. Keep your mobile phone on with a well charged battery!

Take your time – and pray through before completely letting go of your heart. If you begin to feel a lack of peace at any stage, pull back, slow down and inquire both from the Holy Spirit – and your friend, what the matter is. Do not advance in the friendship until you have received cogent assurances from the Lord. If your *inner* peace is troubled at any time, wait until any matters arising are resolved!

God may readily arrange other avenues other than *go-between's* and internet sites through which you may meet your future spouse. In the Old Testament, each of the patriarchs of the faith met their spouses after much intercession to God. Some met besides a well; others, on farmlands where they worked. A few had met by word of mouth – having been introduced or suggested by someone else! The *well* symbolizes the place of living waters. That would translate to a living church; a God-related program like friends' wedding ceremonies, christian house warming, birthday celebrations, in a supermarket aisle, on a train *etcetera*. Do not place a limit and a cap on which route the Father could chose to take.

Be expectant.

Be alert!

Be ready!!

Above all, make yourself available!!!

4. Build a Substitute Altar unto the LORD

The last instruction the Lord issued Gideon was to:

> *"Build an altar unto the Lord thy God ... and offer a burnt sacrifice with the wood of the grove which thou shalt cut down."*

JUDGES 6:26

What a compulsive command! The reason for the compulsion, you would agree, was justified. Simply, God's expectations of and qualification standards to *any* willing to inherit His promises will not be compromised. [23] Your nationality, racial, academic or economic status has nothing to do with influencing the mind of God!

In Luke 9:23 we hear of the non-negotiable terms of discipleship from the lips of the Savior:

> *"And he said to them all, If any man will come after me, let him deny himself, and take up his cross daily, and follow me."*

The key phrase is *deny himself.*

You see, Jesus' terms are anything but straightforward – and strict! In other words, The Master Discipler says: *"I demand you discipline your members; intentionally refuse your selfish interest any chance to master you. Do not indulge in gratifying the demands of your lower nature."*

Our Master's high expectation of us is to follow Him daily and cleave unto, conforming unto His lifestyle in the face of the pressures to conform to the sinful *self!*

We have seen the set of strategic but impulsive commands God laid on Gideon. Gideon would have to atone for *his* personal sins first before becoming eligible to atone for the wrongdoings of his generation. Then Baal altar must be overthrown. The shade-giving trees of the grove must be uprooted so as to let new, liberating light of God's truth percolate the soil of the hearts. Finally, a brand new altar must be raised!

In a parallel move, when Elijah, the prophet of God had confronted Baal – a false god, which nonetheless, had become a national epidemic in Israel – and his 450 false prophets; Elijah, like Gideon would have to repair and rebuild the altar of God which Baal's prophets had damaged while they frantically called to him in prayers. [24]

Jesus' words are pertinent to our understanding of the moves by God's servants to rebuild the altar of

Baal! The Savior says:

> *"No man putteth a piece of new cloth unto an old garment …*
>
> *Neither do men put new wine into old bottles: else the bottles break, and the new wine runneth out, and the bottles perish: but they put new wine into new bottles, and both are preserved."*

MATTHEW 9:16-17

This interprets that if we really thirst for the move of God in our nations, our personal lives must first re-focus on God. Also, we would necessarily re-dedicate and re-align our lives to the things of God and His Spirit.

For example, if you've never yielded your life in obedience to Christ, God cannot use you! You're *the* old wine; the new wine of the Spirit cannot be poured into *you!* Necessarily, now is the accepted time. This is in accordance with building a new acceptable altar of new sacrifice unto the Lord God of Heaven, the only true God!

We have identified the 'groves' of our modern time – and thankfully, we know what to with them, don't we? Mandatorily, garbage corrupting materials such as erotic DVD's, magazines, novels and books would be disposed away from our domains. When you are disposing off such, it would be recommended that you not offer them to another person! You could call on your Pastor or Deacon's Board for help to rightly dispose them on your behalf. If you are unchurched, you may offer a safe bon-fire night wherein these offensive and demonic materials are burnt up. Visits to pornographic sites will be completely banned because restrictive new filters to which you have no pass codes are being enforced. You would do well also to be accountable to a faithful and trusted friend or leader at Church. These suggestions are approved safe 'detox' strategies for someone like you.

Also, old cargo friends and companies that have kept you bound will have to be jettisoned overboard! Remember, whatever has not added unto your life must have been deducting from you!

Be Warned!

Before you get overjoyed with your deliverance, let me sound you a note of caution. Be warned! Demons and demonic altars do not let go of their old captives without giving a tough fight – and staging a renaissance, a re-grouping and a re-entry bid for a re-possession!

As many as had had one dealing or another with the spiritual forces of wickedness must take to heart, Jesus' warning in Matthew 12:43–45:

> *"When the unclean spirit is gone out of a man, he walketh through dry places, seeking rest, and findeth none.*

Then he saith, I will return into my house from whence I came out; and when he is come, he findeth it empty, swept, and garnished.

Then goeth he, and taketh with himself seven other spirits more wicked than himself, and they enter in and dwell there: and the last state of that man is worse than the first. Even so shall it be also unto this wicked generation."

Your yielded obedience to Christ will yield *the* key to unlocking the potentials embedded within your very fabrics; albeit, in gradual turns!

Chapter 6

Work-in-Progress

"Where sin abounded, grace did much more abound."

- APOSTLE PAUL

Work-in-Progress is an accounting term used in the manufacturing industries. The importance of *Work-in-Progress* goods in the final assessment of any Manufacturing/Trading Company's Profit and Loss Account, Balance Sheet – and other final Books of Account must not be under emphasized, if the company would not run bankrupt.

Work-in-Progress goods simply, are goods in the transient stage of production upon which huge investments and outlaid pre-paid costs have been incurred. *W.I.P* goods are *finished products* awaiting deft, finishing touches!

Father God is the Potter. Scripture teaches we are His handiworks. [1] We were fabricated – among the entirety of His handiworks – for the sole display of His glory:

> *"For we are God's (own) handiwork (His workmanship) recreated in Christ Jesus ... that we may do those good works which God predestined ..."*

EPHESIANS 2:10, AMP

Of a truth, we are God's investments on earth! God secured our eternal worth through the eternal sacrifice on the Cross of His only begotten Son, Jesus Christ.

> *"For God so loved the world, that he gave his only begotten Son, that whosoever believeth in him should not perish, but have everlasting life."*

JOHN 3:16

If You Are Not At Your Very Best

Each sinner knows deep down within themselves that, given their present circumstances evidenced by their lifestyles, they are not at the very best the Creator fashioned them out for in His original blueprint. Like the characteristic 'Work in Progress' good, they are far from perfection! Perhaps, just a rousing temper, disobedience, lust or ir-reverence keeps them falling short of the grace of God. Their lives keep turning in and out of turmoil!

Friend, roller-coasting in and out of turmoil isn't the Creator's original intent for your life. You can surrender your life to the Prince of Peace today – and make peace with God! Listen, you do not have an eternity to ponder on what you will do with Him called Christ. Quite the contrary; we are told our lives are like vapor that appears for just a little while and then vanishes away. [2]

Satan's Works-in-Regress

The Bible categorically teaches about the remuneration of sin. Romans 6:23 states: *"The wages of sin is death."* But we are also told of God's priceless gift unto us. God's inestimable gift to us is *"eternal life through Jesus Christ our Lord."*

Very simply, it follows then, that if any man refuses God's gift, he automatically accepts Satan's *benefits.* There is no room for coasting along in neutral gear, in the things pertaining to the spiritual realm! The wages of sin is death! Those wages could be quick, sudden judgment or remuneration. Be assured, there is a *pay day!*

For the righteous saved by Christ Jesus, his/her *pay day* is something to look forward to with utmost yearning! For the ungodly, their *pay day* is going to be a day of God's wrath!

Some others' remunerative 'pay day' would *not* be quick and sudden! It will be gradual *death-in-process;* that is, death by installment.

Ponder upon this list which by no means is exhaustive of Satan's 'work in regress': poverty, disease, unfathomable illnesses and afflictions; torments, seizures, shame, insanity, fear, barrenness, stagnation and failure. Any of these is as morbid as real death. Some other death-invoking *benefits* on Satan's *reserve bench* include fear, indebtedness, dumping projects, incurable diseases, ancestral/generational curses and the workings of evil covenants upon a person, family, generation or nation!

How would you know if what you are currently experiencing is one of Satan's Works-in-Regress?

You would know by asking if the particular problem had ever occurred to someone or more, in *your* lineage. Be candid with your evaluation.

You see, we recognize Satan's strategy of destruction because he specializes in the perpetuation of an evil over a lineage over time. Realistically then, you must realize you have a battle to fight! Please, do *not* allow the penalties of sins committed by some unknown but related person(s), group(s) or ancestor(s) rest on your destiny.

Gideon, puzzled by the ancestral inherited curses upon his generation demanded from the angel of the Lord:

> "Oh my Lord, if the LORD be with us, why then is all this befallen us? and where be all his miracles which our fathers told us of ... ?"

JUDGES 6:13

God's response to Isaiah, faced with similar agitation is recorded:

> *"Behold, the LORD's hand is not shortened, that it cannot save; neither his ear heavy, that it cannot hear:*
>
> *But your iniquities have separated between you and your God, and your sins have hid his face from you that he will not hear."*

ISAIAH 59:1–2

The people of Gideon's day did not even think it grave the evil they committed unrestrained. Their hearts had become dulled by sin! God's wrath manifested.

However, a sensitive heart is God's delight, for we read:

> *"A broken and contrite hear; Oh God thou wilt not despise."*

PSALMS 51:17

One man's sins got him paralyzed for thirty-eight years until the day he encountered Jesus Christ the Savior, who *"went about doing good and healing all that were oppressed of the devil."* [3] Jesus had compassion on him, and healed him.

The Lord however warned him to *"sin no more, lest a worse thing come unto thee."* [4]

Your disobedience to God it is that have held you

down, defeated for so long! Once sin is sown into operation, and is not repented of, its effects will undoubtedly manifest – in no time! This is what eventually causes us trouble on earth – and *the* after-life in hell!

God's Grace in Process

You need not suffer death, hell and judgment! You need not heap upon yourself God's wrath. Jesus' eternal blood, shed for you, is *God's-Grace-in-Process*.

God demonstrates His eternal love for His erring handiwork, by laying down His only begotten Son's life – and pouring out His precious blood, as *the* final atoning act of grace. The Bible assures us: *"the blood of Jesus Christ; his Son cleanseth us from all sin."* [5]

God sent His only begotten Son, Christ Jesus to die in *your* stead – and mine! It was His shed blood, for instance, that atoned for my sins. This was what made me right with God.

> *"For without the shedding of blood there is no remission of sins."*
>
> HEBREWS 9:22

Jesus' precious blood, shed, absolves the sinner totally from their sins.

This same blood paved the way for *my* redemption, reconciliation, restoration renewal and security with *my* Creator. I am at peace with God today not because I am a preacher; nor any other reason besides the Blood of Jesus Christ, the Blood of atonement, shed for me.

Apply the Blood

If only you would repent of your sins – and renounce them before God now, Jesus' blood will transform you into a new child of God! You will be redeemed, restored, renewed, forgiven and made secure with Father God. Apply this Blood: it will bring you home. It is written – *"But now in Christ Jesus ye who sometimes were far off are made nigh by the blood of Christ."* [6]

God extends to you His invitation of love:

> *"Come now, and let us reason together, saith the LORD: though your sins be as scarlet, they shall be as white as snow; though they be red like crimson, they shall be as wool."*
>
> ISAIAH 1:18

If God has spoken to your heart even now, and you would want to appropriate the blood of Jesus to make you a new creature; then, pause a while, bow your head and pray this prayer aloud with me:

"Dear LORD Jesus,

I know that I am a sinner. I know that the sentence of God's wrath looms over my destiny. I want you to know that I am deeply sorry for my sins.

I want – and do ask for your forgiveness. I ask that the blood of Jesus Christ cleanse me, from this day.

I ask to be released from the penalties of my sins – as You came to pay for the eternal consequences of my sins upon the Cross through Your sufferings, death, burial and resurrection!

Deliver me, Father God, from your wrath, judgment and hell. Please make me your child now; write my name in the Lamb's Book of Life.

I have prayed in the name of Jesus Christ, my Savior!

Amen!

Signed & Dated

If you prayed that prayer, kindly write me today to:

Sammy Joseph Ministries
Box 15129, Birmingham
England, B45 5DJ

Or please address your email to *reverendsammy@harvestways.org*

I love you –
and would be looking forward to hearing from you!

Simply Free

Congratulations! You are now a Blood-bought Child of the Most High God! Welcome to *your* very first breath of freedom – in an eternity-long freedom in Christ.

We read in John 8:36 the words of our LORD:

> *"If the son therefore shall make you free, you shall be free indeed."*

Receive, in faith, the words of the Lord as having accomplished your destiny. This is the *first* step to unfurling God's manifold grace unto you.

Your *second* step forward is to:

> *"Stand fast therefore in the liberty wherewith Christ hath made us free, and be not entangled again with the yoke of bondage."*

GALATIANS 5:1

Move forward in faith.

Grow in your new found liberty in the Lord's name, outgrowing all forms of weaknesses as you submit unto the Lordship of Jesus Christ.

Find a true Bible believing Church where you will be taught the undiluted Word of God.

Settle down to learn how to *metamorphorsize* into Heaven's Work-in-Progress, ready for Heaven's advertisement, display and use (2 Timothy 2:20–21).

If the Lord lays it upon your heart to worship with

us, we will welcome and celebrate you. Therefore, you may have a look at any of our addresses closest to you and join us. As you get committed to God, God will get committed to you.

I commit your spirit, soul and body *"unto him that is able to keep you from falling and to present you faultless before the presence of his glory with exceeding joy."* (Jude 24)

Congratulations!

References

Chapter 1

[1] Philippians 4:13

Chapter 2

[1] 1 Chronicles 4:9–10
[2] Revelations 12:11
[3] John 9:2-3
[4] Deuteronomy 12:8
[5] Numbers 23 & 2 Peter 2:14–16
[6] Ephesians 4:19
[7] 1 Timothy 4:2
[8] Matthew 16:18–19
[9] Acts 24:27
[10] Romans 1:5; Amplified Version
[11] 3 John 2

Chapter 3

[1] Judges 6:6
[2] Exodus 2:25

3. *1 Chronicles 4:10*

4. *Mark 10:47*

5. *Mark 10:52*

6. *Judges 6:8*

7. *Luke 1:18-22*

8. *PULSE Magazine, Vol. 1 No. 2; 1996. Copyrighted.*

9. *2 Kings 13:21*

10. *Ephesians 2:20*

11. *Matthew 7:24-27*

12. *2 Kings 5:9-14*

13. *2 Kings 13:16*

14. *Exodus 17:9-13*

15. *1 Kings 12 & 2Kings 23*

16. *Matthew 7:20*

17. *Matthew 22:36-39*

18. *Matthew 7:15-23*

19. *Colossians 3:5*

20. *1Corinthians 14:3*

21. *1 Kings 8:63-9:3*

22. *Acts 12:20-24*

23. *Acts 4:12*

24. *Hebrews 1:14*

25. *PULSE Magazine, Testimony. Vol. 4 No. 4; Nov. 2000. Copyrighted.*

26. *Revelations 5:18 & Philippians 4:18*

27. *Esther 4:16*

28. *Daniel 3:17-18*

29. *Mark 8:35*

30. *Daniel 6:7*
31. *Acts 12:1-11*

Chapter 4

1. *Genesis 32:25*
2. *Galatians 6:17*
3. *Galatians 4:9*
4. *Judges 8:32*
5. *Philippians 1:15-18*
6. *Romans 8:30*
7. *Ecclesiastes 10:19*
8. *James 3:15*
9. *1 John5: 4*
10. *Judges 6:27*
11. *Judges 6:5*
12. *Ezekiel 37:12*
13. *Ezekiel 37:4*
14. *Ezekiel 37:9*
15. *Proverbs 18:21; Amplified Version*
16. *Isaiah 48:11*
17. *Psalms 20:7-8*
18. *1 Timothy 4:15*
19. *Hebrews 8:6*
20. *Luke 5:1-11*

Chapter 5

1. *Deuteronomy 30:19; Amplified Version.*

2. *1 Corinthians 9:27*

3. *2 Corinthians 10:6*

4. *Matthew 6:10*

5. *Psalms 40:6-8*

6. *Ephesians 4:23*

7. *1 Samuel 15:9*

8. *2 Corinthians 8:8*

9. *2 Corinthians 8:10-15*

10. *Acts 13:22*

11. *1 Samuel 16:7*

12. *Psalms 68:6*

13. *Collins Concise Dictionary, 21st Century Edition; 5th edition, 2001.*

14. *Ephesians 2:2, emphasis; mine*

15. *Ephesians 5:21*

16. *Judges 6:27*

17. *Matthew 7:3-5*

18. *Ephesians 6:1*

19. *Psalms 81:9*

20. *Ephesians 3:10*

21. *John 10:3; Amplified Version*

22. *A British Broadcasting Corporation's Outlook Report, 2000*

23. *Romans 2:11*

24. *1 Kings 18:1-46*

Chapter 6

1. *Jeremiah 18:6*

2. *James 4:14*

References

3. *Acts 10:38*
4. *John 5:5-14*
5. *1John 1:7b*
6. *Ephesians 2:13*

Worship with Us

**The Harvestways Int'l Church,
(Birmingham, U.K.)**

Holloway Community Hall,
Northfield, Birmingham
England, United Kingdom B31 1TT
Sundays: 12 noon- 2pm
Fridays: 7–8.30pm (House Fellow-
ship)
Tel: (+44) 7906441276
(+44) 7854675159

**The Harvestways Int'l Church
(South Africa)**

Eindhoven Primary School Hall
Eindhoven Delft South 7100
Capetown,
South Africa
Sundays: 9am – 11am
Wednesdays: 6pm
Mobile: (+27) 7436 55011
(+27) 732454884

**The Harvestways Int'l Church
(Nigeria, West Africa)**

1 Harvest Way, Off Elewura Street
Behind Zartech / GLO Office,
Challenge G.P.O Box 2910
Dugbe, Ibadan Oyo State,
Nigeria, West Africa.
Sundays: 9am
Wednesdays: 6pm
Mobile: (+234) 8078198576
(+234) 8023928508

You may want to inquire about SJM,
invite Rev. Sammy to minister for you
or become a partner; please contact:

Sammy Joseph Ministries
P.O. Box 15129,
Birmingham,
West Midlands,
England
B45 5DJ
Mobile: (+44) 7906 441276
(+44) 7854 675159

Other Books by the Author

Other books by the author that can be ordered at all Christian bookshops near you, *Pulse Publishing House* or from our website *www.harvestways.org* include:

BEFORE YOU STEP INTO SOMEONE ELSE'S SHOES

This book contains *easy-to-do* guides on how you will not repeat the costly mistakes made by others faced with a fresh opportunity to begin anew after suffering a heavy setback. We have also provided essential checklists to anyone willing to *step into shoes* ordained of God for them – as well as checkmating the mutineers!

DESTROYING THE POWER OF DELAY

Best seller expository piece of writing. The author aims at showing you how to avoid the path that leads to a detour of destiny; 22 major causes of delay; how to maximally profit in delay and virtues that will enable you enter into and abide in your destiny.

Download *PULSE On-line*, freely at *www.harvestways.org*

Contact Addresses

United Kingdom

The Harvestways Int'l Church
Holloway Hall, Ley Hill
Birmingham
England
B31 1TT

United Kingdom

Sammy Joseph Ministries
Box 15129
Birmingham,
England, U.K
B45 5DJ
Tel: (+44) 7906441276
(+44) 7854675159

Nigeria
Pulse Publishing House
Plot 1, Harvest Way
Behind GLO Office
Challenge
G.P.O. Box 2910
Dugbe
Ibadan
Nigeria.
Mobile: (+234) 8136812070

South Africa
Pulse Publishing House
351 Delft Main Road
Delft South
Capetown
South Africa
7100
Mobile: (+27) 7436 55011
(+27) 732454884

*On-line availability @ www.harvestways.org,
WHSmith.com, & Barnesandnoble.com*